# Viral
# Social
# Media
## Growth Blueprint

Proven Methods to Build Your Brand and
Generate Revenue on Facebook, TikTok,
Instagram, X(Twitter) and YouTube and
Attract  a Massive Audience

## CHAD SCOTT

# TABLE OF CONTENT

# Introduction

In today's digital world, social media has become more than just a way to connect with friends and family. It's now one of the most powerful tools for personal branding, business growth, and financial success. Whether you're a budding content creator, an entrepreneur, or someone who wants to make a bigger impact, social media offers you a global stage to grow your influence.

But standing out in the crowd of millions of users isn't easy. It takes more than posting occasionally or sharing a few photos. To truly succeed, you need a strategic approach that turns your followers into a loyal community, and your content into viral gold. This book is designed to be your step-by-step guide to achieving that. Whether you're starting from scratch or looking to refine your strategy, you'll find actionable advice and proven methods that will help you grow your social media presence and unlock new opportunities.

We'll explore the latest strategies that successful influencers and businesses are using in the US, from mastering Instagram Reels and TikToks to building engaged audiences on YouTube and X (formerly Twitter). Along the way, you'll learn how to create content that resonates, leverage platform algorithms to your advantage, and ultimately turn your social media growth into real-world success.

# Foreword

Social media is no longer just a tool for entertainment—it's a gateway to influence, success, and even financial freedom. Platforms like Instagram, TikTok, and YouTube have given rise to a new generation of entrepreneurs and influencers, many of whom are making six or seven figures by leveraging their online following. This phenomenon isn't limited to celebrities or big brands. Everyday people, from small-town creators to stay-at-home parents, are building substantial audiences and turning their passions into profitable ventures.

Take, for example, the rise of Charli D'Amelio on TikTok. In just a couple of years, she went from an unknown teen in Connecticut to one of the most recognizable names in social media. With consistent posting, viral dance challenges, and an authentic connection with her audience, Charli became the first TikTok star to surpass 100 million followers, leading to brand deals with major companies like Dunkin' Donuts and launching her own products.

Or consider MrBeast (Jimmy Donaldson), whose viral YouTube videos have not only made him a millionaire but also allowed him to launch philanthropic efforts that have garnered millions of views and donations. His approach to content—combining massive giveaways, stunts, and community involvement—turned his channel into a global phenomenon.

These examples show that with the right strategy, anyone can go viral, grow their influence, and open doors to new opportunities. Whether you're promoting a business, building a personal brand, or looking to connect with a larger audience, social media offers limitless potential. But it requires more than just luck. Success in social media comes from understanding how to play the game: creating content that resonates, engaging with followers, and staying ahead of trends.

This book will break down exactly how you can do that. By the end of it, you'll be equipped with the tools and knowledge to grow your social media presence in a way that leads to real influence and success.

# Part 1

# Laying the Groundwork for Social Media Success

# Chapter 1

## Crafting Profiles, Bios, and Branding That Stand Out

Your social media profile is your digital storefront—it's the first impression people get of who you are and what you represent. In the few seconds it takes someone to land on your page, you need to communicate your brand, personality, and why they should stick around. This is why crafting an engaging profile, writing a compelling bio, and establishing a strong personal or business brand is crucial to your social media success.

In this chapter, we'll break down how to create profiles, bios, and branding that not only stand out but also convert casual visitors into followers and loyal fans.

### The Importance of a Strong First Impression

Imagine walking into a store with no signage, confusing layouts, and no clear indication of what's being sold. You'd likely leave in seconds. Social media is the same. When users land on your page, they quickly assess if it's worth following. A polished, professional-looking profile sets you apart from the millions of other accounts, giving you instant credibility.

Take Instagram, for example. Your profile picture, bio, and highlighted stories are all visible before a person ever scrolls through your content. These elements need to immediately communicate your message. Whether you're an entrepreneur looking to promote your products or a content creator hoping to grow your following, first impressions matter.

### Crafting the Perfect Profile Picture

Your profile picture is often the first thing people notice. It should be clear, on-brand, and professional. If you're a personal brand, a well-lit, high-quality headshot works best. For businesses, use your logo or a clean, branded image that represents your values.

Let's look at one of the most followed figures on social media: Gary Vaynerchuk, an entrepreneur and motivational speaker. His profile picture across platforms—whether on Instagram, Twitter, or LinkedIn—is consistent. It's a close-up, smiling headshot that communicates professionalism but also approachability, key to his brand.

For businesses, take Nike as an example. The company uses its iconic swoosh logo consistently across all platforms, ensuring that users recognize the brand instantly.

**Tips for a Strong Profile Picture:**
- Use a high-resolution image.
- Ensure the picture is well-lit and not overly cluttered.
- Keep it simple and professional.
- Stay consistent across all platforms (Instagram, Facebook, TikTok, etc.).

## Writing a Bio That Grabs Attention

Your bio is a snapshot of who you are or what your brand offers. It's where visitors decide if your content aligns with their interests. A great bio is concise, clear, and engaging. It should convey your value proposition—what makes you unique and why someone should follow you.

**Key Elements of a Strong Bio:**
- **Clarity:** Make it immediately clear who you are and what you do.
- **Value:** Explain what followers will get out of following you. Are you offering tips, entertainment, or inspiration?
- **Call to Action (CTA):** Encourage visitors to take the next step, whether that's following you, visiting your website, or signing up for a newsletter.

**Example of a Clear Bio (Personal Brand):**
*"Helping entrepreneurs grow their businesses through social media strategies. Follow for daily tips and inspiration. ■: [email address]."*

**Example of a Clear Bio (Business):**
*"High-quality, eco-friendly apparel. Shop our latest collection 🌿■."*
*(With a link to the shop)*

In both examples, the bios are short, punchy, and include a call to action. They tell the audience exactly what to expect, making it easier for people to hit that follow button.

## Branding: Establishing Your Unique Voice and Aesthetic

Branding is more than just your logo or color scheme—it's about the consistent message you convey through your visuals, tone, and content. Successful branding tells a story about your values and mission, making it easier for people to connect with you.

Take a look at how personal finance expert Dave Ramsey brands himself across platforms. His posts, bio, and tone are consistent across Instagram, Twitter, and Facebook. His branding is all about no-nonsense, practical advice for getting out of debt and building wealth. The same applies to influencers like fashion blogger Aimee Song, whose visual branding consistently reflects minimalism and elegance.

## How to Develop Your Brand:

- **Define Your Values:** What do you want to stand for? Whether it's authenticity, humor, or motivation, your brand should align with the core message you want to communicate.
- **Pick Your Aesthetic:** Are you bold and colorful or more minimal and refined? Your color scheme, fonts, and image styles should be consistent across platforms.
- **Craft Your Tone:** Whether you're educational, entertaining, or inspirational, your tone of voice should be consistent in your captions, posts, and videos.

## Consistency Across Platforms

One of the most important aspects of building a recognizable brand is consistency. If someone follows you on TikTok and then finds you on Instagram, they should be able to recognize your profile immediately. That means using the same profile picture, similar bios, and maintaining a consistent posting style across all platforms.

Consistency helps build trust, making your audience feel they're following someone reliable and professional. For example, U.S.-based entrepreneur Jenna Kutcher maintains her brand aesthetic across Instagram, her podcast, and even her website. Her audience knows exactly what to expect from her: empowering, creative content for female entrepreneurs.

## Optimizing Your Profile for Each Platform

While consistency is key, it's also important to tailor your profiles to the specific platform you're using. Each platform has its own strengths, and your profile should be optimized accordingly.

- **Instagram:** Focus on visually appealing content. Use stories and highlights to showcase your best work or key aspects of your brand. Instagram allows for a brief bio, so make it count with a clear message and a CTA.
- **TikTok:** Your bio should quickly communicate what type of videos people can expect from you. Since TikTok is all about short-form content, make sure your bio reflects the energy of your videos.
- **X (Formerly Twitter):** Your bio needs to be even more concise, given the platform's fast-paced nature. Use it to quickly explain your niche or expertise.

- **YouTube:** Since YouTube allows longer bios, you can go into more detail about your content, but still lead with the value you offer to viewers.

Your social media profile is the foundation of your success. A well-crafted profile picture, a clear and compelling bio, and a consistent brand message are what separate you from millions of others. By taking the time to set up your profile correctly, you're setting yourself up for long-term growth and success.

In the next chapter, we'll dive into how to identify your ideal audience so you can tailor your content to the people most likely to engage with and share it, driving your social media growth.

# Chapter 2

## Finding Your Tribe

If you try to appeal to everyone, you'll end up resonating with no one. Social media success comes from deeply understanding your audience—knowing who they are, what they care about, and how your brand fits into their lives. This chapter will walk you through how to identify your ideal audience and build a personal brand that speaks directly to them.

### Why Finding Your Audience is Crucial

Think of your audience as your "tribe." These are the people who not only follow you but also resonate with your content, engage with your posts, and ultimately help you grow by sharing your message. Identifying your ideal audience is the foundation of creating content that goes viral. The more targeted your content, the more likely it will hit home with the right people—those who will like, comment, share, and advocate for you.

Take the example of fitness influencer Chloe Ting, who's built a massive following by targeting a specific niche: people looking for quick, at-home workouts. She understood that her ideal audience was time-conscious individuals looking to stay fit without a gym membership, and she tailored her content to meet their needs.

## Identifying Your Ideal Audience: Who Are They?

To grow your social media presence, you first need to understand who you're speaking to. Identifying your ideal audience involves analyzing their demographics, behaviors, interests, and pain points. Here's how to get started:

**1. Demographics:**
- What is their age range?
- Where are they located?
- What is their gender identity?
- What is their income level?
- What is their education level?

**2. Psychographics:**
- What are their interests and hobbies?
- What are their core values?
- What motivates them?
- What social media platforms do they use the most?

### 3. Pain Points:
- What challenges or problems do they face that your content or brand can solve?
- What are their goals, desires, and aspirations?

**Example:** Imagine you're a personal finance coach. Your ideal audience might be U.S.-based millennials between the ages of 25-35 who are struggling with student debt and looking to improve their financial literacy. Knowing this, you can create content around budgeting tips, debt management, and investing for beginners, using platforms like Instagram and YouTube where this demographic is highly active.

**Pro Tip:** Use social media analytics tools to gather information about who's currently engaging with your content. Tools like Instagram Insights, Facebook Analytics, and TikTok Pro offer data on your followers' age, location, and activity, helping you refine your ideal audience.

## Building a Personal Brand That Speaks to Your Tribe

Once you've identified your ideal audience, the next step is to build a personal brand that appeals to them. Your personal brand is more than just your logo or tagline—it's the overall perception your audience has of you. It's how you present yourself, your tone of voice, your values, and the emotional connection you create.

Here's how to build a personal brand that resonates:

**1. Authenticity:** Be real and relatable. People are drawn to authenticity. Whether you're documenting your entrepreneurial journey or sharing behind-the-scenes glimpses of your life, let your audience see the real you. For example, U.S.-based entrepreneur Gary Vaynerchuk is known for his no-nonsense, raw approach to documenting his business strategies. This authenticity is central to his brand and is a big reason for his success.

**2. Consistency:** Whether it's your messaging, tone, or visuals, be consistent across all your platforms. When your audience knows what to expect from you, it builds trust and makes your content recognizable. Look at brands like Nike, which uses a consistent tone of inspiration and motivation across their Instagram, Twitter, and TikTok accounts.

**3. Storytelling:** People connect with stories. Whether it's sharing your journey, how you overcame obstacles, or the values that drive you, storytelling makes your brand more relatable and memorable. For instance, skincare brand Glossier built its brand on authentic stories from real users, rather than relying solely on traditional advertising.

**4. Emotional Connection:** Successful personal brands tap into their audience's emotions. Think about what emotions you want to evoke. Do you want to inspire? Entertain? Educate? Brands like Disney do this masterfully by creating content that evokes nostalgia and joy, drawing people into a deeper emotional connection.

### Niche Down for Bigger Growth

It might seem counterintuitive, but narrowing your focus can actually lead to bigger growth. By niching down, you create a clear identity that attracts your ideal audience more effectively than trying to be everything to everyone.

For example, beauty influencer Huda Kattan built her empire by focusing specifically on makeup tutorials and beauty products for women of color—a niche that was underrepresented in the beauty industry. As her brand grew within this niche, her influence expanded globally.

When you define a niche, your content becomes more focused, making it easier for the right people to find you and for you to become an authority in that space.

**Steps to Niche Down:**
1. Identify a specific problem or interest within your broader topic.
2. Research whether there's demand within that niche (through social media hashtags, groups, forums, etc.).
3. Tailor your content to address that niche specifically, ensuring that you're offering unique value.

## Connecting with Your Audience: Engagement is Key

Social media is a two-way street. To truly grow your audience, it's not enough to simply post great content—you also need to engage with your followers. Building relationships with your audience is what turns passive followers into an active community that supports and promotes your brand.

Here are some key ways to boost engagement:

- **Respond to Comments:** Whether it's replying to a compliment or addressing a question, responding to your followers creates a personal connection.
- **Ask for Feedback:** Use polls, questions, and surveys to ask your audience what they want to see more of. This not only boosts engagement but also gives you insights into their preferences.
- **Go Live:** Platforms like Instagram, TikTok, and YouTube allow you to interact with your audience in real-time. Going live to answer questions, provide tips, or simply chat with your followers creates an authentic connection.

**Example:** Take YouTube fitness influencer Whitney Simmons. She frequently responds to her followers' comments and questions, making her audience feel valued and heard. This engagement fosters a strong community, leading to higher retention and loyalty.

### U.S.-Based Case Study: Building a Tribe with Targeted Content

Let's consider the case of entrepreneur Pat Flynn, the founder of Smart Passive Income. Flynn built a highly engaged audience by consistently targeting aspiring entrepreneurs in the U.S. who wanted to create passive income streams. He provided valuable, actionable content specific to this niche, including podcasts, blogs, and YouTube videos, while building trust through engagement and transparency.

Through targeted content, authentic storytelling, and consistent branding, Flynn grew a tribe of loyal followers who resonate deeply with his message, proving that understanding and connecting with your audience is key to long-term success.

Your ideal audience is out there waiting to connect with you. By identifying who they are, crafting a personal brand that speaks to them, and actively engaging with them, you can create a loyal community that not only follows you but also helps you grow through shares, likes, and recommendations. In the next chapter, we'll dive into how to create viral content that resonates with your tribe and keeps them coming back for more.

# Chapter 3

# Creating Attention-Grabbing Content

In a world where people scroll through their social media feeds at lightning speed, creating attention-grabbing content is an essential skill. Whether you're writing a blog, crafting a social media post, or designing visuals, understanding the psychology of what captures attention and compels people to engage is key to your success.

In this chapter, we'll explore the science behind creating content that stops the scroll, engages your audience, and keeps them coming back for more.

### The Anatomy of a Viral Post: Understanding Attention Triggers

Before diving into the specifics of different types of content, it's important to understand what drives attention on social media. Every viral post—whether it's a tweet, Instagram image, or TikTok video—leverages certain psychological principles to capture and maintain attention. These triggers can be boiled down to four core components:

**1. Emotion:** Content that triggers an emotional response—whether it's joy, surprise, or even anger—is more likely to be shared. For example, heartfelt posts that inspire, motivate, or make people laugh are more likely to go viral.

**Example:** A 2020 TikTok by Nathan Apodaca (@420doggface208) went viral after he filmed himself skateboarding while drinking cranberry juice and lip-syncing to Fleetwood Mac's Dreams. The feel-good vibe and authenticity of the video sparked a wave of recreations and even drew attention from the band themselves.

**2. Relevance:** Content that feels directly relevant to the audience's lives or current events grabs attention. Staying on top of trends and creating posts that tie into them—like holiday events, news stories, or viral challenges—can give your content a viral boost.

**3. Novelty:** The human brain is wired to notice things that are new or different. Whether it's a surprising fact, a fresh take on a familiar topic, or a visually unique design, novelty can grab attention and make people stop scrolling.

**4. Visual Appeal:** Social media is a visually-driven environment, and high-quality visuals are often the first thing people notice. Bold colors, eye-catching images, and well-designed layouts can significantly increase the likelihood that people will engage with your content.

## Writing Blogs that Convert: Structure, Headlines, and Readability

When it comes to writing blogs that engage readers, structure and clarity are key. Blogs remain a powerful tool for establishing authority, driving traffic to your website, and building a loyal audience—but only if your readers actually stick around long enough to read them.

**Headline:** The headline is arguably the most important part of your blog post. Studies show that 8 out of 10 people will read your headline, but only 2 out of 10 will read the rest. A great headline is short, specific, and conveys a clear benefit.

**Example:** Instead of "How to Get More Followers," a stronger headline would be, "5 Proven Strategies to Gain 1,000 Followers in 30 Days."

**Introduction:** Hook your readers in the first few sentences by addressing a common pain point or offering a surprising fact. The introduction should clearly explain why the reader should keep reading and what they'll gain from the post.

**Body:** Break up your content into easy-to-digest sections using subheadings, bullet points, and short paragraphs. This improves readability and keeps readers engaged. For example, a blog post on how to create viral TikTok videos might include sections on video length, sound selection, and using captions effectively.

**Call-to-Action (CTA):** Every blog should end with a CTA, whether it's encouraging readers to share the post, sign up for your newsletter, or leave a comment. This keeps engagement high and drives readers toward the next step.

### Crafting Social Media Posts: The Art of Captions and Short-Form Content

On platforms like Instagram, TikTok, and Twitter (now X), captions are often just as important as visuals. In a few words, you need to convey value, invite engagement, and, ideally, spark a conversation.

**1. Keep It Short and Sweet:** The ideal length for social media posts varies by platform, but in general, shorter is better. Twitter (X) limits you to 280 characters, which forces you to be concise. On Instagram and TikTok, while you have more space, shorter captions often perform better because they're easier to digest.

**Example:** Fitness influencer Kayla Itsines uses short, punchy captions on her Instagram posts to engage her audience, such as: "Let's smash this workout! What's your go-to move?"

**2. Ask Questions or Use CTAs:** Asking your audience questions or giving them a clear call-to-action can encourage engagement. For example, you might ask, "What's your favorite way to stay productive? Comment below!" This not only drives comments but also signals to the algorithm that your post is generating engagement, increasing its reach.

**3. Use Emojis Strategically:** Emojis can help break up text and add a fun element to your posts, but don't overdo it. Use emojis that match your brand tone and support your message.

**4. Harness Trending Hashtags**: On platforms like Instagram and TikTok, hashtags are crucial for expanding your content's reach. Use a mix of trending and niche-specific hashtags to make your content discoverable. Tools like Hashtagify or Instagram's explore feature can help you find the right ones

## Visuals That Pop: The Psychology of Color, Design, and Imagery

Visual content is the backbone of platforms like Instagram, TikTok, and Pinterest. But creating visuals that stand out requires more than just pretty pictures—it's about understanding what elements draw the eye and keep attention.

**1. Color Psychology:** Different colors evoke different emotions. Red can create a sense of urgency or excitement, while blue is calming and conveys trust. Understanding the psychology of color can help you choose a palette that aligns with your brand and message.

**Example:** U.S.-based tech YouTuber Marques Brownlee (MKBHD) uses a sleek, modern design with bold colors in his thumbnails, making his videos instantly recognizable.

**2. Consistency is Key:** Use consistent fonts, colors, and design elements across all your visuals to create a cohesive look that's easily associated with your brand. Many influencers, like @thebucketlistfamily, use consistent filters and layouts to create a unified Instagram feed, which helps build brand recognition.

**3. Simplicity Over Complexity:** When it comes to visual content, less is often more.

Don't overwhelm your audience with too many elements. A clean, simple design is easier to process and more likely to grab attention.

**4. The Rule of Thirds:** This is a classic design principle that suggests dividing an image into thirds (both vertically and horizontally) and placing the most important elements along these lines or at their intersections. This creates a balanced, visually appealing composition.

### U.S.-Based Case Study: How BuzzFeed Creates Viral Visual Content

BuzzFeed has mastered the art of creating viral content by leveraging the power of visuals. Their listicles and quizzes are not only fun and shareable but are also visually engaging. Each post is carefully designed with eye-catching colors, bold fonts, and well-placed images that draw users in.

For example, BuzzFeed's "Which U.S. City Should You Actually Live In?" quiz went viral thanks to its blend of engaging visuals and a fun, relatable topic that resonated with its audience. The quiz's shareable format also encouraged users to post their results on social media, helping it gain even more visibility.

## Creating Content for Today's Platforms: TikTok, YouTube, and X

TikTok: Short, snappy, and highly visual, TikTok is all about trends and creativity. Successful TikTok content often incorporates music, quick transitions, and trending challenges. Aim for videos that are 15-60 seconds long and use TikTok's editing tools to keep things dynamic.

**Example:** TikToker @brittany_broski gained millions of followers by jumping on trends while staying authentic and humorous, which resonates with her Gen Z audience.

**YouTube:** Long-form content thrives on YouTube. Whether it's tutorials, vlogs, or deep dives into specific topics, YouTube allows creators to build a strong connection with their audience through informative, entertaining content. Thumbnails and titles play a crucial role in attracting viewers, so make sure they're designed to pique curiosity.

**X (Formerly Twitter):** The key to success on X is staying concise and timely. Tweets that perform well tend to be topical, witty, and engage with trending conversations. Use hashtags and mentions to get your tweets seen by a wider audience.

Creating attention-grabbing content is a blend of art and science. By understanding the psychological triggers behind viral content and tailoring your blogs, posts, and visuals to meet these triggers, you can create content that not only stops the scroll but also engages your audience deeply.

In the next chapter, we'll dive into how to build a consistent social media presence and grow your community with engagement strategies and content calendars.

# Chapter 4

# Mastering Visual and Viral Video Storytelling

In today's digital world, visuals speak louder than words, and nothing connects faster with audiences than engaging visual content. Whether you're using photos, memes, or short-form videos on TikTok and Instagram Reels, mastering the art of visual storytelling is essential to growing your social media presence.

In this chapter, we'll explore how to create compelling visual content that resonates with your audience, with a focus on the specific platforms where it can go viral.

## The Power of Visual Storytelling

Visual storytelling taps into our brain's natural tendency to process images faster than text. A single photo or video can evoke emotions, spark curiosity, or tell a complex story in seconds. This makes visuals a powerful tool for social media growth, especially on visually-driven platforms like Instagram, TikTok, and Pinterest.

What makes visuals so powerful? Here are a few reasons:

**1. Instant Impact:** We process images 60,000 times faster than text. This makes photos and videos particularly effective at grabbing attention.

**2. Emotional Connection:** Visuals have the ability to evoke emotions instantly. Whether it's joy, sadness, excitement, or curiosity, strong emotions often lead to shares and increased engagement.

**3. Universality:** A well-crafted image or video can cross language barriers, making visual content highly shareable across global audiences.

### Mastering Photos for Social Media

Although short-form videos are becoming increasingly popular, photos are still foundational for platforms like Instagram and Pinterest. But to stand out in a sea of selfies and scenic shots, your photos need to tell a story or elicit a strong reaction.

Here are some tips to create visually compelling photos:

**1. High-Quality Imagery:** Whether you're using a smartphone or a professional camera, your images need to be clear and high-quality. Blurry, poorly lit photos won't grab attention in crowded feeds.

**Example:** On Instagram, photographer Brandon Woelfel (@brandonwoelfel) creates stunning portraits with vibrant lighting and unique compositions, making his work instantly recognizable.

**2. Composition Matters:** Use photography techniques like the rule of thirds to create balanced, visually appealing images. Consider framing, leading lines, and symmetry to guide the viewer's eye and add depth to your photos.

**3. Tell a Story:** A single photo can tell a story if it's thoughtfully crafted. Think about the emotions, message, or narrative you want to convey. For example, lifestyle photos that show behind-the-scenes moments or candid shots tend to perform well because they feel more relatable.

**4. Edit for Impact:** Don't underestimate the power of editing. Use tools like Lightroom or VSCO to adjust lighting, enhance colors, and sharpen your photos. Many U.S.-based influencers like @tezza (Tezza Barton) have signature editing styles that help establish their personal brand.

## Memes: The Language of the Internet

Memes have become a form of modern communication, spreading like wildfire across social media platforms. They're funny, relatable, and designed to be shared—which makes them a great tool for growing your audience.

**1. Relatability is Key:** The most successful memes tap into shared experiences or universal feelings. Whether you're commenting on a popular trend or poking fun at a common frustration, the more relatable your meme is, the more likely it is to be shared.

**Example:** Memes about work-life balance or "Monday blues" often go viral because they resonate with a broad audience.

**2. Leverage Trending Formats:** Memes often follow specific formats or templates, and jumping on these trends can help you tap into a larger conversation. Websites like Know Your Meme can help you stay up-to-date with the latest meme trends.

**3. Simplicity Wins:** Memes are meant to be quickly consumed. Use minimal text and keep your images simple. Overcomplicating a meme can dilute its message.

## TikToks and Reels: Short-Form Video Mastery

Short-form videos have taken over social media, with TikTok and Instagram Reels leading the way. These platforms prioritize creative, bite-sized content that hooks viewers in seconds and encourages them to share, comment, and recreate your content.

Here's how to create viral-worthy videos for TikTok and Reels:

**1. Jump on Trends:** TikTok is driven by trends, whether it's a popular sound, challenge, or hashtag. If you can creatively incorporate a trend into your niche, your video is more likely to go viral.

**Example:** The "Renegade" dance challenge, originally from TikTok, swept across the platform and became a global sensation. Brands and creators alike jumped on this trend to increase visibility.

**2. Capture Attention in the First Few Seconds:** You have just 3 seconds to grab your viewer's attention. Start your video with a hook—something surprising, funny, or visually engaging. For example, use a bold statement, an eye-catching visual, or an unexpected action.

**3. Use Music to Your Advantage:** On TikTok, music and sound play a huge role in video performance. Trending songs often get boosted by the algorithm, so incorporating popular sounds can help increase your reach. Instagram Reels follows a similar pattern, with viral sounds boosting visibility.

**4. Editing and Transitions Matter:** On both platforms, editing is key. Quick cuts, transitions, and creative effects can make your video more dynamic and engaging. TikTok and Instagram both have built-in editing tools that are easy to use, allowing you to add music, effects, and text.

### U.S.-Based Case Study: How Charli D'Amelio Built a Brand on TikTok

Charli D'Amelio, one of TikTok's biggest stars, gained millions of followers by mastering the art of short-form video storytelling. Her rise to fame started with participating in viral dance challenges, but what set her apart was her relatable personality and consistent engagement with trends. By tapping into the platform's most popular content while staying authentic, Charli became one of the most recognizable influencers in the U.S.

**Lessons from Charli's Success:**
**1. Consistency:** Charli posted frequently, ensuring she stayed at the top of TikTok's algorithm and her followers' feeds.
**2. Trends + Authenticity:** While she participated in trending challenges, she added her unique flair, making her content feel authentic.
**3. Engagement:** Charli interacted with her followers, responding to comments and doing "duets" with other creators, which helped build a strong community around her brand.

## Turning Stories into Movement: Creating Visual Content with a Purpose

In addition to entertainment, visual storytelling can also be used to create movements and inspire change. Social media activism has become a powerful force, and many influencers and brands use their platforms to promote causes and spark conversations around important issues.

Here's how to create meaningful visual content that can go viral:
**1. Align with a Cause:** Choose a cause that resonates with your audience and aligns with your values. Whether it's social justice, environmental sustainability, or mental health, authenticity is key. U.S.-based movements like

#BlackLivesMatter gained traction on social media by leveraging powerful imagery and video to spread awareness.

**2. Use Emotional Imagery:** Visual content that evokes strong emotions—such as powerful photos, thought-provoking memes, or heartfelt videos—tends to be shared more.

**3. Create a Call to Action**: Encourage your audience to participate in the movement by sharing your content, using a specific hashtag, or taking a specific action. For example, the ALS Ice Bucket Challenge encouraged people to post videos of themselves completing the challenge, which led to millions of shares and donations.

Visual storytelling is more than just creating pretty pictures or fun videos—it's about connecting with your audience on a deeper level and delivering a message that resonates. Whether you're posting photos, memes, TikToks, or Reels, the key to success is understanding the emotions and psychology that drive engagement.

In the next chapter, we'll dive into strategies for leveraging platform-specific tools and techniques to boost visibility and grow your audience even further.

# Part 2

# Growing Your Social Media Presence on Key Platforms

# Chapter 5

# Instagram and Facebook Growth: From 0 to Millions of Engaged Followers

Growing a massive, engaged following on social media platforms like Instagram and Facebook requires more than just posting frequently. It's about creating a deep connection with your audience, utilizing the latest platform features, and leveraging strategies that attract the right people. This chapter will take you step by step through the strategies and techniques used by some of the most successful social media influencers and brands to go from zero to millions of engaged followers.

## Understanding Instagram and Facebook Audiences

To build a massive following, it's important to first understand the core differences in the audiences and engagement styles on Instagram and Facebook.

**Instagram:** Primarily a visual platform, Instagram's audience tends to be younger, with a large concentration of users aged 18-34. People use Instagram to discover trends, brands, and influencers, making it ideal for growth if you can master eye-catching visuals and relevant content.

**Facebook:** With a more diverse user base that spans multiple age groups, Facebook has a broader reach and allows for more in-depth engagement through posts, comments, and long-form content. Facebook's Groups and Pages are key to building loyal communities, which is crucial for long-term follower growth.

## Optimizing Your Profiles for Growth
## 1. Profile Pictures, Bios, and Branding:
Your profile on both platforms is the foundation of your online presence. Make sure your profile picture is consistent and professional across platforms. Whether you use a logo or a headshot, it should be clear and reflective of your brand.

**Instagram Bio:** Your bio should tell people exactly who you are, what you offer, and why they should follow you. Use a compelling call to action and include relevant keywords. Adding links to your website, a free resource, or other social media channels can also drive engagement.

**Facebook Bio:** Since Facebook allows for more text, take advantage of the space in the "About" section to provide detailed information about your brand, services, and mission. You can also include links to groups or other pages you manage to funnel traffic and build a community.

## 2. Consistent Visual Branding:

Your visual aesthetic is just as important as your written content. Instagram is all about curated feeds, and Facebook posts with images receive higher engagement. Create a consistent color palette, fonts, and design style for your posts so that your audience recognizes your content instantly.

## Crafting Content That Attracts Millions
## 1. Posting High-Engagement Content:

Both Instagram and Facebook algorithms reward posts that drive engagement (likes, comments, and shares). Here's how to create posts that can get millions of interactions:

## Instagram Content Strategies:

- Post content that resonates emotionally with your audience—whether it's inspirational, humorous, or informative.
- Use Stories and Reels to engage followers with behind-the-scenes content, tutorials, or trends.

- On Instagram, a mix of high-quality photos, carousel posts (multiple images), and Reels will boost visibility.

**Facebook Content Strategies:**
- On Facebook, longer posts can perform well, especially those that start conversations or share valuable information. Personal stories, behind-the-scenes insights, and controversial topics often trigger high engagement.
- Use Facebook Live for real-time interactions with followers and post videos regularly. Facebook prioritizes video content, especially live streams.

**2. Engaging Captions and Calls to Action:**
Your captions are the key to engagement. Rather than simply describing your photo or video, use captions to start conversations. Ask questions, encourage people to share their thoughts, and use strong calls to action like "double tap if you agree" or "tag a friend."

**3. Hashtags and Geotags:**
Hashtags can help new audiences discover your content. On Instagram, use a combination of popular and niche hashtags to maximize reach. Aim for a mix of branded, community, and trending hashtags. On Facebook, hashtags are

less critical but can still help make content discoverable.

**4. Timing Matters:**
Posting at the right times ensures your content reaches the largest number of followers when they're most active. In the U.S., research suggests that the best times to post on Instagram are around 9 AM and 11 AM, while Facebook engagement spikes around 1 PM to 3 PM. However, always experiment with different times to see what works best for your specific audience.

## Growing Your Following: The Secrets Behind Massive Growth

### 1. Collaborations and Shoutouts:
Collaborating with other creators, brands, or influencers is one of the fastest ways to grow. Cross-promotion exposes you to their audience and vice versa. This can be done through guest posts, shoutouts, co-hosted events or live streams, and influencer marketing.

**Example:** Many U.S. brands collaborate with influencers on Instagram to promote their products in exchange for a shoutout, which instantly puts their account in front of thousands (or even millions) of new eyes.

## 2. Contests and Giveaways:

Contests can quickly boost your follower count. Encourage your audience to tag friends, share your posts, or follow your account for a chance to win something valuable. This strategy works incredibly well on both Instagram and Facebook and can result in exponential growth if executed well.

**Example:** A simple giveaway offering a free product or gift card can generate thousands of new followers overnight. Just make sure the prize is relevant to your audience.

## 3. Engaging in Trends and Challenges:

Participating in trending challenges on Instagram and Facebook can get your content in front of a much larger audience. Use popular music or memes in Reels and Stories to ride the wave of viral content.

**Example:** TikTok challenges often spill over onto Instagram Reels and Facebook, allowing you to tap into a larger, viral trend.

### Paid Strategies for Explosive Growth

While organic growth is ideal, paid advertising can be a powerful tool for speeding up the process.

**1. Instagram Ads:**
Instagram Ads are highly customizable, allowing you to target specific demographics, interests, and behaviors. To get the most out of Instagram Ads:

- Use engaging, high-quality visuals or video content that captures attention within the first few seconds.
- Create targeted campaigns to reach specific audience segments, such as U.S.-based users who are interested in your niche.

**2. Facebook Ads and Boosted Posts:**
Facebook's advertising platform is one of the most powerful in the world. You can create ads that target specific age groups, geographic areas, interests, and even behaviors. Boosting posts can also help increase reach and engagement for content that's already performing well organically.

## Case Study: From 0 to Millions—How a U.S. Influencer Did It

**Case Study:** Huda Kattan (Instagram Handle: @hudabeauty)

Huda Kattan, a beauty influencer based in the U.S., grew her Instagram following to over 50 million by sharing beauty tips, tutorials, and product reviews. She consistently used high-quality visuals, engaged personally with her followers, and built a strong personal brand that resonated with her audience.

**Key Takeaways:**
- **Consistency is Key:** Huda posts daily, ensuring that her followers always have fresh content to engage with.
- **Engagement with Followers:** She regularly responds to comments and interacts with her audience in her Stories, which helped foster a sense of community and loyalty.
- **Leveraging Instagram Stories and Reels:** Huda uses Instagram's Stories and Reels to provide behind-the-scenes insights and viral beauty hacks, both of which have helped her maintain visibility in a crowded market.

Going from zero to millions of engaged followers on Instagram and Facebook requires time, effort, and strategic planning. By focusing on high-quality content, engaging your audience, collaborating with others, and using both organic and paid strategies, you can build a massive and loyal following. Remember that the key is not just in the number of followers but in building a community that values and interacts with your content consistently.

In the next chapter, we'll explore strategies for growing on TikTok and YouTube, two platforms that have become crucial for viral video content and personal branding.

# Chapter 6

# TikTok Fame and YouTube Success

TikTok and YouTube have become the go-to platforms for anyone looking to achieve viral fame and long-term success. Both platforms offer unique opportunities to build a following by tapping into trends, creating short-form content, and capitalizing on viral movements. This chapter will guide you through the key strategies for growing your presence on TikTok and YouTube, using real-world examples and insights into how the latest trends can skyrocket your content to millions of views.

### Why TikTok and YouTube Matter for Personal Growth

### 1. TikTok's Explosive Reach:

TikTok has reshaped social media by providing a platform where users can go viral overnight. The algorithm is designed to push content from smaller creators as long as it's engaging, giving everyone an equal chance to gain visibility. In the U.S. alone, TikTok has millions of users who consume content across all niches, from education to entertainment.

## 2. YouTube's Longevity and Discoverability:

YouTube, on the other hand, is a platform with lasting power. Videos uploaded to YouTube can generate views for years, thanks to its search engine capabilities. YouTube Shorts, a feature designed to compete with TikTok, also makes it easier to create viral content and attract new subscribers with short, engaging videos.

## TikTok: Tapping into Trends and Challenges for Viral Fame

TikTok is driven by trends, challenges, and short-form video content. The platform's "For You" page (FYP) curates content based on user interests and behavior, allowing your videos to reach users who don't already follow you.

## 1. Leveraging TikTok Trends:

One of the easiest ways to go viral on TikTok is by participating in trending challenges or using trending sounds. By jumping on a trend early, you can increase your chances of your content being featured on the FYP.

**Example:** A U.S. makeup artist gained over 500k followers by participating in the "Euphoria makeup challenge" at the height of the show's popularity. She used trending sound clips and visually stunning makeup transitions, which caught the attention of users outside her normal reach.

## 2. Creating Authentic, Relatable Content:
TikTok users are drawn to authenticity. Unlike Instagram, where content is often curated and polished, TikTok thrives on genuine, raw, and even imperfect content. Share behind-the-scenes moments, everyday experiences, or insights into your personal journey to connect with your audience on a deeper level.

## 3. Consistent Posting Schedule:
Posting frequently is essential for TikTok growth. Because of the platform's fast-paced nature, it's recommended to post at least once per day. This increases your chances of landing on the FYP and gaining followers quickly.

**YouTube:** Building a Loyal Subscriber Base with Short and Long-Form Content
YouTube offers more versatility when it comes to content length, and balancing both short-form (YouTube Shorts) and long-form videos is the key to success.

**1. YouTube Shorts:** The Shortcut to Viral Growth
YouTube Shorts, similar to TikTok, are 60-second vertical videos designed for quick

consumption. Since its introduction, many creators have experienced viral growth by posting Shorts regularly.

**Example:** A fitness trainer in the U.S. grew her channel from 5k to over 100k subscribers by posting daily workout Shorts that appealed to busy professionals. Her most popular Short, a 15-second ab workout, garnered over a million views and brought her significant new traffic.

**2. Long-Form Videos:** Building Depth and Authority
While Shorts bring new followers, long-form content is where you can establish authority and build a loyal community. Tutorials, vlogs, how-tos, and personal stories allow you to dive deeper into subjects that matter to your audience.

**Example:** A tech reviewer who consistently posts detailed reviews of new gadgets has built a loyal subscriber base because his followers trust his in-depth insights and analysis.

**3. Utilizing SEO and Keywords for Discoverability**
YouTube is the second-largest search engine in the world. To make sure your videos are discoverable, use relevant keywords in your titles, descriptions, and tags. Do keyword

research to find out what your target audience is searching for, and create content that answers their questions or addresses their interests.

## How to Hook Your Audience with Short-Form Content

**1. Grabbing Attention in the First 3 Seconds:** Both TikTok and YouTube Shorts rely on capturing attention quickly. The first three seconds of your video are critical—whether it's an eye-catching visual, a question that piques curiosity, or a bold statement. Hook your viewers immediately to stop them from scrolling.

**Example:** Many viral TikTok creators start their videos with an intriguing question, such as "Did you know this life hack?" or with a dramatic visual that grabs attention right away.

**2. Storytelling and Emotional Hooks:**
Even in short-form content, storytelling is key. Whether you're sharing a funny anecdote, an inspiring story, or a quick tip, structure your video with a clear beginning, middle, and end. Emotional hooks—such as humor, surprise, or inspiration—help your video stand out and make it more shareable.

## Riding the Wave of Viral Movements and Trends

### 1. Viral Challenges and Hashtags:

Both TikTok and YouTube Shorts benefit from viral challenges. By incorporating popular hashtags and challenges into your content, you can dramatically increase your chances of being seen.

**Example:** On TikTok, the #bussitchallenge was one of the most viral trends in recent history. Creators from all niches participated, and those who put their unique spin on it saw their videos go viral.

### 2. Music and Sound Effects:

Using trending music or sound bites in your videos can significantly boost engagement, particularly on TikTok. TikTok's algorithm favors content that incorporates trending sounds, and the platform makes it easy for users to find videos using a specific sound.

## Collaborating with Other Creators to Multiply Growth

### 1. Cross-Promotions and Collaborations:

Collaborating with other creators in your niche is one of the fastest ways to grow. Whether it's doing a duet on TikTok, guest appearances on each other's YouTube channels, or collaborating on challenges, cross-promotion exposes your content to a new audience and boosts your visibility.

**Example:** U.S. lifestyle influencers often collaborate on TikTok by doing duets or reaction videos, which helps them tap into each other's follower base. Similarly, YouTube creators collaborate by appearing in each other's vlogs or co-hosting challenges.

## 2. Influencer Collaborations:
Working with influencers can also give your content a significant boost. Identify creators in your niche who have large followings and engage in collaborative efforts like shoutouts, giveaways, or shared videos.

### Case Study: TikTok to YouTube Stardom—The Journey of Charli D'Amelio

Charli D'Amelio's rise to fame on TikTok is the perfect example of how consistency, relatability, and leveraging trends can lead to viral success. Charli began by posting dance videos on TikTok, quickly participating in trending challenges and making use of popular music.

### Key Takeaways:
- **Consistency:** Charli posted content daily, often multiple times per day, which kept her in front of the audience regularly.

- **Leveraging Trends:** By participating in TikTok's most popular challenges, she increased her visibility and reached millions of viewers.
- **Expansion to YouTube:** Once Charli gained traction on TikTok, she expanded her brand to YouTube, where she now has millions of subscribers who engage with her longer, more personal content.

TikTok and YouTube offer endless opportunities to build a large and engaged following if you leverage trends, produce high-quality short-form content, and engage authentically with your audience. By tapping into viral movements, using SEO strategies, and collaborating with other creators, you can grow your presence and become a well-known name in your niche.

In the next chapter, we'll dive into how to use X (formerly Twitter) and LinkedIn to grow your influence, focusing on real-time engagement and professional networking. These platforms may not be as visually-driven as TikTok and YouTube, but they are essential for building authority and expanding your reach across different audiences.

# Chapter 7

# Real–Time Growth on X (Twitter) and LinkedIn

While platforms like TikTok and YouTube emphasize visual content and trends, X (formerly Twitter) and LinkedIn offer unique opportunities for real-time engagement, professional networking, and building thought leadership. This chapter will explore strategies to grow your presence on these platforms, focusing on creating meaningful connections, participating in real-time conversations, and establishing yourself as a credible voice in your industry.

## The Power of Real-Time Engagement on X (Twitter)

X, still commonly known as Twitter, thrives on real-time conversation. It's a platform where ideas, news, and trends spread rapidly, giving you the opportunity to join conversations that matter and position yourself as an expert in your niche.

## 1. Building a Personal Brand on X:

The key to growth on X is consistent engagement. Unlike Instagram or YouTube, X relies on short, concise posts that can be seen by a large audience if timed right. To build a strong presence, focus on these strategies:

**Stay Topical:** Engage with trending topics and hashtags relevant to your industry. Whether you're in tech, health, or entertainment, join ongoing conversations to get noticed by a broader audience.

**Example:** In the U.S., entrepreneurs like Elon Musk use X to share quick updates on new ventures, thoughts on the future of technology, and even personal musings. This keeps them constantly in the public eye and generates organic growth through retweets and replies.

## 2. Crafting the Perfect Tweet:

Tweets that resonate are those that are informative, engaging, and sometimes witty. Use clear, impactful language to deliver your message quickly, and always include a call to action (CTA) to encourage interaction.

**Example:** A popular financial expert grew their following by tweeting short, actionable investing tips. By focusing on relevant topics (e.g., stock market trends) and including CTAs such as "Retweet if you're investing in your future," they quickly built a community of engaged followers.

### 3. Twitter Threads and Long-Form Content:

While X is known for its brevity, Twitter Threads allow you to share more in-depth content. Create value-packed threads that offer tips, guides, or stories that resonate with your audience. Threads are especially useful for establishing authority in a particular field and can go viral with the right approach.

**Example:** U.S. entrepreneurs often use threads to share the behind-the-scenes stories of their startup journeys, which not only humanizes them but also inspires their followers.

### 4. Real-Time Interaction and Viral Engagement:

One of X's biggest advantages is its real-time nature. You can engage with trending topics and breaking news as it happens, which allows you to gain visibility through relevant discussions.

**Example:** During major events like the Super Bowl or award shows, brands and influencers jump into the conversation with witty commentary or viral memes, boosting their engagement instantly.

## LinkedIn: Building Authority and Professional Networks

LinkedIn, often thought of as a more traditional platform, is crucial for anyone aiming to build a professional brand. It is a space to establish authority in your field, share industry knowledge, and network with like-minded professionals.

### 1. Optimizing Your LinkedIn Profile for Personal Branding:

Your LinkedIn profile serves as a digital résumé and personal branding tool. To stand out, ensure that your profile reflects your expertise, credibility, and unique value proposition.

**Professional Headline and Summary:** Craft a concise headline that highlights what you do and how you help others. In your summary, share your story—why you're passionate about your field and what unique experiences you bring to the table.

**Example:** A U.S. marketing consultant might use a headline like "Helping startups scale with data-driven marketing strategies," followed by a summary that shares their personal journey and key achievements.

**2. Posting Long-Form Content for Engagement:**
Unlike X, LinkedIn is a platform where users expect and engage with long-form content. Regularly post thought leadership articles, case studies, or tips in your niche to build credibility and attract followers.

**Example:** A business leader in the tech industry might post detailed articles on emerging AI trends or strategies for remote leadership, drawing the attention of professionals and industry insiders.

**3. Engaging with the LinkedIn Community:**
LinkedIn is more than just a platform for posting content—it's a place to foster meaningful conversations. Engage with other professionals by commenting on their posts, joining industry groups, and participating in discussions.

**Example:** A career coach who regularly engages with posts about leadership development can gain visibility and build a network of professionals looking for guidance, eventually leading to more clients or collaborations.

## Cross-Promotion: How X and LinkedIn Work Together

Leveraging X and LinkedIn simultaneously can amplify your message across different audiences. While X allows for quick, real-time updates, LinkedIn gives you the space for more thoughtful and professional content.

### 1. Cross-Promoting Content:

If you write a long-form post or article on LinkedIn, share a snippet of it on X with a link to drive traffic back to your LinkedIn profile or post. This helps funnel your X audience to your more in-depth LinkedIn content.

**Example:** A digital marketing expert might post a thread on X with quick tips on social media growth, then link to a full article on LinkedIn that dives deeper into those strategies.

### 2. Expanding Your Professional Reach:

Since LinkedIn caters to professionals and X reaches a wider range of audiences, cross-promotion helps you maintain relevance in both spheres. Use LinkedIn to establish authority and X to participate in broader cultural or industry-related conversations.

## Hashtags and Trends: Leveraging Algorithms for Growth

### 1. Using Hashtags on X:

Hashtags on X help categorize your tweets and allow them to be discovered by users following or searching those topics. Follow trending hashtags, but also create your own hashtags related to your niche to encourage others to join the conversation.

**Example:** A U.S. entrepreneur could use hashtags like #Entrepreneurship or #SmallBusinessSuccess when sharing insights about their journey, making it easier for others in the space to find and engage with their content.

### 2. LinkedIn Hashtags for Discoverability:

Hashtags on LinkedIn function similarly to those on X but are more industry-specific. Include a few relevant hashtags in your posts to increase your visibility among professionals in your field.

**Example:** A U.S.-based leadership coach might use hashtags like #LeadershipDevelopment, #ExecutiveCoaching, or #CareerGrowth to reach an audience specifically interested in those topics.

# Thought Leadership on LinkedIn: Building Influence Over Time

## 1. Establishing Expertise:

Consistently sharing industry insights, engaging with others, and posting original content helps establish you as a thought leader. Over time, this builds a reputation that attracts followers, connections, and opportunities for collaboration.

**Example:** A U.S. digital transformation expert could regularly post about the latest innovations in cloud computing or AI, which attracts the attention of decision-makers in the tech industry.

## 2. LinkedIn Articles and Newsletters:

LinkedIn allows you to publish longer articles and even newsletters directly on the platform. Use this feature to create in-depth content that addresses pressing issues or shares valuable insights with your audience.

**Example:** A finance professional might publish a weekly newsletter on LinkedIn covering market trends, investment strategies, and financial tips. This positions them as a go-to expert in their field.

## Real-Time Conversations and Thought Leadership: Timing is Everything

### 1. Timing Your Tweets on X for Maximum Engagement:

To grow your audience on X, it's essential to post when your target audience is most active. Pay attention to time zones and the times when engagement typically spikes, such as early mornings, lunch breaks, or evenings.

### 2. LinkedIn's Best Posting Practices:

On LinkedIn, posts tend to perform best during business hours, especially on weekdays. Keep your audience in mind when scheduling posts to ensure that they see your content when they're most likely to engage with it.

## Case Study: Building Personal Influence on X and LinkedIn

### Example:

A U.S. business consultant combined daily engagement on X with weekly articles on LinkedIn to grow their influence in the entrepreneurship space. On X, they shared quick tips and real-time thoughts on the startup world, while on LinkedIn, they provided more detailed case studies and industry insights. By leveraging both platforms effectively, they built a diverse following of engaged professionals and entrepreneurs.

X and LinkedIn are powerful tools for building both personal influence and professional authority. By participating in real-time conversations on X and providing thought leadership on LinkedIn, you can grow a robust and engaged audience. In the next chapter, we'll explore how to create viral movements and collaborations with influencers to further expand your social media presence across all platforms.

# Chapter 8

# Building a Loyal Community

One of the most crucial aspects of social media growth is building a loyal and engaged community. It's not enough to just have followers; you need to foster a sense of belonging and excitement that turns casual viewers into superfans. Superfans are followers who not only consume your content but actively promote it, engage with you regularly, and form a community around your brand or personal presence. This chapter focuses on the strategies you can use to create that community and maintain consistent interaction.

## Why Engagement Matters More Than Followers

Many aspiring social media creators focus primarily on the number of followers they have, but engagement is a far more valuable metric. It's better to have 10,000 engaged followers than 100,000 passive ones. Engagement leads to deeper relationships, stronger communities, and eventually more conversions if you're offering products, services, or promoting content.

**Example:** A fitness coach on Instagram might have 30,000 followers, but because they reply to comments, share follower content, and host regular Q&A sessions, they have an engagement rate of over 10%, leading to better brand loyalty and product sales.

### Responding to Comments: The Foundation of Engagement

It may seem simple, but responding to comments is one of the most powerful tools for building a loyal community. When followers see that you're actively engaging with them, they feel more connected to you, and this encourages others to join the conversation.

**Tip:** Personalize your responses. Instead of replying with a generic "Thank you!" try to include the follower's name and add a question or thought that encourages more discussion.

**Example:** An influencer in the U.S. food blogging scene responds to each comment on their recipe posts with cooking tips, alternative ingredients, or even just appreciation for the comment, which helps build a strong, loyal audience who feels valued.

## Creating Interactive Content to Boost Engagement

One of the best ways to encourage consistent interaction is by making your content interactive. This includes asking questions, hosting polls, and creating challenges that invite your audience to participate. People love to share their opinions and experiences, and this drives engagement while also providing valuable insights into your audience's preferences.

**Polls and Q&A Sessions:** Instagram Stories, TikTok, and Twitter (X) offer easy ways to ask your followers questions and get real-time feedback.

**Example:** A U.S.-based fashion influencer might use Instagram polls to ask followers to choose between two outfits, generating engagement and providing insights into what their audience prefers.

**Challenges and User-Generated Content:** Challenges, especially on platforms like TikTok and Instagram, allow you to create viral movements within your community. Encourage your followers to create their own versions of your content and share it with a specific hashtag.

**Example:** A fitness trainer could launch a 30-day workout challenge, encouraging their followers to share daily progress using a branded hashtag. This not only engages current followers but also exposes the brand to new audiences.

### The Power of Live Interaction: Instagram and TikTok Live

Live videos create a sense of immediacy and intimacy, making them a powerful tool for building deeper connections with your audience. On platforms like Instagram Live, TikTok Live, and YouTube Live, you can directly answer questions, share exclusive content, and interact with viewers in real-time. This makes your audience feel more connected to you and your brand.

**Example:** A U.S. wellness coach regularly hosts Instagram Live sessions where they discuss mental health tips, take questions from followers, and offer personal advice. These sessions build trust and make followers feel like they're part of a supportive community.

**Best Practices for Live Sessions:**
- Promote your live event ahead of time to ensure a good turnout.

- Keep the session interactive by responding to comments, answering questions, and even inviting followers to join the live feed.
- Offer exclusive content, such as behind-the-scenes looks or announcements, that isn't available anywhere else.

**Building Loyalty Through Consistency**
Consistency is key when it comes to building a loyal community. Followers come to expect regular content from you, and delivering on those expectations helps keep them engaged. Develop a content calendar and stick to it, whether you post daily, weekly, or bi-weekly.

**Example:** U.S.-based entrepreneurs on LinkedIn often post updates every Monday to start their week with fresh insights, giving their followers a reliable source of knowledge to look forward to.

**Tip:** Make use of content scheduling tools like Hootsuite or Buffer to ensure you stay consistent with your posting, even during busy periods.

### Nurturing Superfans: Going the Extra Mile
Superfans are the core of your loyal community. These are the followers who go out of their way to comment on every post, share your content,

and promote you to their own followers. To build superfans, you need to go above and beyond in nurturing those relationships.

**Reward Your Superfans:** Show appreciation for your most engaged followers by acknowledging them in your posts, offering exclusive content, or hosting giveaways that reward loyal followers.

**Example:** A beauty influencer might feature their superfans in their Instagram Stories, thanking them personally for their support. This kind of recognition fosters a strong sense of loyalty.

**Exclusive Access:** Offer your superfans something exclusive that other followers don't get. This could be early access to content, special discount codes, or even a private Q&A session.

**Example:** A U.S. tech influencer might invite their most engaged followers to a private webinar or release exclusive content, giving them a sense of belonging to an inner circle.

## Creating a Sense of Community Among Followers

Creating a community means fostering interaction not just between you and your followers, but among your followers themselves. Use your platforms to encourage followers to connect with each other, share stories, and offer support.

**Facebook Groups and Online Communities:** Build a dedicated space where your most engaged followers can interact with each other. Facebook Groups or private Discord channels are great for this, as they create a sense of exclusivity and community.

**Example:** An online business coach in the U.S. might start a private Facebook group for entrepreneurs where members can share tips, ask for feedback, and collaborate on ideas. This kind of peer interaction strengthens community bonds.

## Case Study: Turning Followers into Superfans

**Case Study:** A U.S.-based lifestyle influencer started with a modest following of 10,000 people but grew to 100,000 highly engaged followers in less than a year. How? They focused on interacting with every comment, hosting weekly live chats, and launching a viral

30-day challenge that encouraged followers to post about their personal growth. By consistently engaging with their audience and rewarding their most loyal followers, they built a community of superfans who promote their content at every opportunity.

Building a loyal community on social media takes time, dedication, and a genuine commitment to engaging with your followers. By focusing on consistent interaction, creating value-packed content, and going the extra mile for your most loyal fans, you'll cultivate a community that actively promotes your growth and success. Superfans are not only your biggest supporters—they're the driving force behind long-term engagement and viral growth.

# Part 3

# The Road to Viral Success

# Chapter 9

# The Secret Sauce to Virality

Going viral is every social media creator's dream, but it's not just about luck. Virality is a result of strategic planning, timing, and understanding what makes content shareable. In this chapter, we'll break down the secret sauce to going viral by exploring the power of trends, hashtags, and creating content that people can't help but share.

## Understanding Virality: What Makes Content Go Viral?

At its core, viral content is content that spreads rapidly across social media platforms because it resonates with a broad audience. This kind of content tends to evoke strong emotions—whether it's laughter, awe, inspiration, or even surprise. When people feel an emotional connection to content, they are more likely to engage with it and share it with their own networks.

- **Example:** A simple yet heartfelt TikTok video of a U.S. veteran reuniting with his family went viral because it tapped into universal emotions of love, sacrifice, and joy, resulting in millions of views and shares across multiple platforms.

## Spotting Trends Early: The Key to Timely Content

One of the best ways to ride the wave of virality is by tapping into current trends. Whether it's a viral dance challenge on TikTok, a trending topic on X (formerly Twitter), or a meme circulating on Instagram, staying ahead of trends can give your content the momentum it needs to go viral.

### How to Spot Trends:

- **TikTok's "For You" Page:** Spend time on TikTok's "For You" page to see which songs, dances, and challenges are gaining traction.
- **X's Trending Topics:** Monitor the trending hashtags and topics on X to see what people are talking about.
- **Instagram Explore Page:** See which kinds of posts and Reels are featured on Instagram's Explore page to get a sense of what's resonating with users.

**Example:** In the U.S., the "Ice Bucket Challenge" became a viral sensation, raising millions for ALS awareness. It started as a small trend but grew as more people participated, demonstrating the power of jumping on a movement early.

## Hashtags: Your Best Friend for Discoverability

Hashtags are one of the most effective tools for increasing the discoverability of your content. They categorize your posts, making it easier for new users to find you through searches and trending topics. But to use hashtags effectively, you need to strike a balance between trending hashtags and niche-specific ones.

### How to Use Hashtags:

- **Trending Hashtags:** Using popular or trending hashtags can expose your content to a larger audience. Be strategic about which ones to use and make sure they're relevant to your content.
- **Niche Hashtags:** These are smaller, community-specific hashtags that may not have as many posts but have a highly engaged audience. They help you target the right people.

**Example:** A U.S.-based food blogger uses a combination of trending hashtags like #foodie and niche-specific ones like #veganrecipes to reach both a broad audience and a highly targeted group interested in plant-based diets.

## Creating Share-Worthy Content: The Emotion Factor

Content that gets shared widely tends to have one thing in common—it triggers an emotional response. Whether it's a funny meme, a heartwarming video, or an inspiring quote, shareable content connects with people on a deeper level. To create content that gets shared, you need to understand what emotions your audience responds to and how to tap into those emotions in an authentic way.

### Key Emotions to Target:

- **Laughter:** People love to share content that makes them laugh. Funny memes, witty captions, and humorous videos are often shared widely.
- **Inspiration:** Motivational content that uplifts people tends to go viral, especially on platforms like Instagram and LinkedIn.
- **Shock or Surprise:** Unexpected content that defies expectations, like plot twists in TikTok stories or surprising statistics, grabs attention and gets shared.

**Example:** A U.S. fashion influencer posted a "before and after" video showing the dramatic difference between a thrifted outfit and a high-end look. The transformation was so impressive that the video quickly went viral, with thousands of shares and reposts.

## Case Study: How a Simple Meme Went Viral

**Case Study:** A U.S. college student created a simple meme comparing the struggles of remote learning to traditional in-class experiences. The meme, which featured relatable images and humorous captions, was shared on X and TikTok and quickly went viral. Within 24 hours, it was reposted by major accounts, featured on news outlets, and received millions of likes and retweets. The key to its success was its relevance to a widespread experience—students adjusting to remote learning during the pandemic—and the relatable humor it conveyed.

## The Power of Challenges and User-Generated Content

Social media challenges have the potential to go viral because they encourage user participation. By creating a challenge, you're not only making engaging content but also inviting your audience to take part in it and share their own versions. This type of user-generated content significantly amplifies your reach.

**Example:** The "Mannequin Challenge," where people froze in place while the camera moved around them, became a viral sensation in the U.S. as thousands of users, including celebrities and brands, participated in the challenge and shared their own videos.

**Tip:** To create your own challenge, come up with an easy, repeatable action or phrase that followers can replicate and make their own. Combine it with a catchy hashtag to track the submissions.

### Leveraging TikTok for Viral Movements

TikTok is perhaps the most powerful platform for going viral today. Its algorithm favors short, engaging, and relatable content, making it easier to reach a massive audience quickly. To go viral on TikTok, focus on using trending sounds, engaging visuals, and participating in viral challenges.

**Example:** In the U.S., a small coffee shop owner gained hundreds of thousands of followers after posting a behind-the-scenes video of their unique coffee-making process. The video, set to a trending TikTok sound, quickly went viral, resulting in a surge of online orders and in-store visits.

## Creating Shareable Infographics and Memes

Infographics and memes are two types of content that are highly shareable, especially on Instagram, Pinterest, and X. Infographics are valuable because they condense a lot of information into easy-to-digest visuals, while memes are great for their humor and relatability.

**Infographics:** Ideal for educational content. Break down complex ideas into simple visuals that can be easily shared.

**Example:** A U.S. health influencer shares infographics on Instagram about healthy eating tips, and the visually appealing format leads to thousands of shares and saves.

**Memes:** Memes capitalize on humor and shared experiences. They're easy to create and share, and when done well, they can generate massive engagement.

**Example:** A meme about the struggles of working from home went viral during the pandemic, as it resonated with millions of remote workers in the U.S.

## Timing is Everything: Posting at the Right Time for Maximum Reach

Even the best content won't go viral if it's posted at the wrong time. Timing plays a crucial role in the success of your post. To maximize your chances of virality, you need to post when your audience is most active.

### When to Post on Different Platforms:

- **Instagram:** Generally, weekdays between 11 AM and 2 PM are optimal times to post.
- **X (Twitter):** Early morning and late evenings tend to have the highest engagement rates.
- **TikTok:** Peak times vary, but evenings and weekends are when most users are active.

**Tip:** Use platform analytics to identify when your followers are most engaged and tailor your posting schedule accordingly.

There is no one-size-fits-all approach to going viral, but by understanding the power of trends, hashtags, emotional connections, and shareable content, you can significantly increase your chances. It's about tapping into what people care about, keeping an eye on the latest trends, and creating content that resonates on a personal level. When done right, your content can capture the attention of the masses and spread like wildfire across social media platforms.

# Chapter 10

# Giveaways and Contests

Running giveaways and contests on social media is a powerful strategy to rapidly increase your follower count, boost engagement, and generate buzz around your brand. Giveaways and contests are particularly effective because they tap into people's desire to win free prizes, creating excitement and encouraging users to interact with your content. This chapter dives into how to plan, execute, and promote giveaways and contests that can significantly grow your social media presence.

## Why Giveaways and Contests Work

Giveaways and contests capitalize on a simple psychological principle: people love free stuff. By offering a valuable prize in exchange for a small action—such as following your account, tagging friends, or sharing a post—you can drastically increase your reach. When done correctly, these campaigns can lead to a surge in followers, heightened visibility, and increased brand loyalty.

**Example:** In the U.S., a small beauty brand ran a giveaway for their latest skincare line.

Participants were required to follow the account, tag three friends, and repost the giveaway on their story. As a result, the brand's follower count doubled in just one week, and engagement on their posts skyrocketed.

**Setting Clear Goals for Your Campaign**
Before launching a giveaway or contest, it's essential to define your goals. What do you hope to achieve? Common goals include:

- **Increasing followers:** Aim to grow your audience by requiring participants to follow your account to enter.
- **Boosting engagement:** Encourage participants to like, comment, and share your content.
- **Promoting a product or service:** Use the contest to build awareness around a new launch or a key product.
- **Generating user-generated content (UGC):** Inspire your followers to create their own content featuring your brand, which you can later share.

**Example:** A U.S.-based fitness influencer launched a challenge-based contest where participants had to upload a video performing a workout routine using a branded hashtag. The campaign resulted in hundreds of user-generated videos, boosting engagement and spreading awareness of the influencer's fitness program.

## Choosing the Right Prize to Attract Your Ideal Audience

The success of your giveaway or contest largely depends on the prize you offer. To attract the right audience, choose a prize that aligns with your brand and appeals to your target demographic. The prize should be valuable enough to motivate users to participate, but also relevant to your niche.

**Types of Prizes:**

- **Products or services you offer:** This not only attracts potential customers but also introduces them to your offerings.
- **Exclusive experiences:** Consider offering something unique, such as a virtual meet-and-greet or a private consultation.
- **Gift cards:** These can appeal to a broader audience and encourage spending within your brand.

**Example:** A U.S.-based fashion boutique ran a contest offering a $500 shopping spree as the prize. This attracted fashion-conscious users and significantly boosted the boutique's follower count among its target demographic.

## Structuring Your Giveaway or Contest for Maximum Engagement

There are many ways to structure your giveaway or contest, depending on your goals. Here are some popular formats:

- **Like and Follow Giveaways:** Participants must like your post and follow your account to enter. This format is simple and great for increasing your follower count.
- **Tag a Friend Contests:** Encourage users to tag friends in the comments for a chance to win. This helps spread your content to a wider audience.
- **Share and Repost Contests:** Ask participants to share or repost your content on their own profiles. This can massively increase your reach and visibility.
- **User-Generated Content Contests:** Encourage users to create content featuring your brand, using a specific hashtag. These contests are excellent for engagement and creating buzz around your brand.

**Example:** A U.S.-based outdoor gear company launched a photo contest, asking participants to share their best hiking photos while using the company's products. The contest generated hundreds of submissions and created a community of engaged outdoor enthusiasts.

## Promoting Your Giveaway or Contest

To ensure your giveaway or contest reaches a wide audience, promotion is key. Use these strategies to get the word out:

- **Leverage Multiple Platforms:** Promote the giveaway on all your social media platforms, such as Instagram, Facebook, TikTok, and X, to maximize exposure.
- **Collaborate with Influencers or Partners:** Partner with influencers or brands in your niche to co-host the giveaway and tap into their followers.
- **Use Paid Ads:** Invest in social media ads to promote your giveaway to a targeted audience. Platforms like Instagram and Facebook allow you to create ads that can extend your reach and bring in new followers.

**Example:** A U.S.-based skincare brand partnered with a popular beauty influencer to promote a giveaway. The influencer shared the contest on their Instagram, and with the influencer's large following, the brand's campaign quickly gained traction, resulting in thousands of new followers.

## Following Legal Guidelines for Giveaways and Contests

Before launching your campaign, it's important to ensure you're following legal guidelines and platform-specific rules. Different platforms have different requirements, so it's crucial to be familiar with them. For example:

- **Instagram:** You must state that Instagram is not involved in the giveaway and that you take full responsibility.
- **Facebook:** You cannot ask participants to share the contest on their timeline as part of the entry requirements.
- **TikTok:** You must disclose any paid partnerships or sponsorships involved in the contest.

Additionally, ensure that your contest rules are clear and transparent. Outline eligibility requirements, how to enter, start and end dates, and how the winner will be selected.

**Example:** A U.S. influencer ran into trouble when their contest didn't follow Instagram's guidelines for disclosing partnerships, resulting in the post being taken down. Always make sure to double-check the rules of the platform you're using to avoid similar issues.

## Announcing the Winner and Keeping the Momentum Going

Once your giveaway or contest has ended, it's important to announce the winner promptly and publicly. This not only builds trust with your audience but also keeps the excitement alive. Consider making the announcement through a post or a live video for added engagement.

**Keeping the Momentum:** After the contest, keep the new followers and participants engaged by immediately offering them valuable content or another promotion. This helps retain the followers you've gained and builds long-term loyalty.

**Example:** A U.S.-based lifestyle blogger hosted a giveaway, and after announcing the winner, they followed up with a special discount code for all participants. This kept the new followers engaged and resulted in increased sales.

## Case Study: How a Giveaway Took a Brand from Unknown to Viral

**Case Study:** A small U.S. wellness brand launched a giveaway offering a wellness retreat as the prize. To enter, participants had to follow the brand, tag three friends, and share the post on their story. The giveaway quickly went viral, with thousands of entries. The brand's follower count skyrocketed from 2,000 to 50,000 within a month, and their engagement rate increased by 300%. This overnight success was due to the valuable prize, strategic promotion, and strong participation incentives.

Giveaways and contests are one of the most effective tools for accelerating your social media growth. By offering something of value, structuring your campaign strategically, and promoting it effectively, you can attract a massive audience, build brand loyalty, and create lasting engagement. When done right, these campaigns can skyrocket your follower count and take your social media presence to new heights.

# Chapter 11

## Live Streaming Mastery

Live streaming has become one of the most powerful tools for creating real-time connections with your audience. Instagram Live, TikTok Live, and YouTube Live each offer unique ways to engage followers, build relationships, and expand your reach. By mastering live streaming, you can increase engagement, foster brand loyalty, and even turn viewers into long-term fans or customers.

In this chapter, we'll explore how to effectively use live streaming to boost engagement, from planning your sessions to interacting with your audience and leveraging each platform's specific features.

### Why Live Streaming Is a Game-Changer

Live streaming allows you to connect with your audience in real time, creating an interactive and personal experience that pre-recorded content can't match. Viewers get to see the unfiltered, authentic version of you, which builds trust and deepens relationships.

**Example:** A fitness influencer in the U.S. uses Instagram Live to conduct real-time workout sessions, offering immediate feedback and answering viewers' questions. This interactive experience keeps viewers engaged and encourages them to return for future live streams, increasing brand loyalty.

**Key Benefits of Live Streaming:**
- **Immediate Engagement:** Real-time comments, questions, and reactions allow you to interact directly with viewers.
- **Authenticity:** Live streaming humanizes your brand, making it more relatable and accessible.
- **Increased Reach:** Most platforms promote live content more heavily than static posts, giving you the opportunity to reach a larger audience.

## Planning Your Live Stream: Timing, Topic, and Purpose

A successful live stream requires careful planning. While spontaneous live sessions can be exciting, structured live streams with clear goals tend to yield better results.

**1. Choosing a Topic:** Focus on content that resonates with your audience's interests. Whether you're sharing a tutorial, conducting a Q&A session, or giving a behind-the-scenes look at your work, make sure the topic aligns with what your audience values.

**Example:** A U.S.-based skincare expert hosts weekly Q&A sessions on TikTok Live, where viewers can ask skincare questions in real time. These sessions have become a popular recurring event, drawing hundreds of viewers each week.

**2. Timing:** Timing is critical for maximizing audience participation. Choose a time when your audience is most active. Most platforms provide insights into when your followers are online, allowing you to schedule your streams strategically.

**3. Purpose:** Define the purpose of each live session. Are you promoting a product, building brand awareness, or simply engaging with your audience? Having a clear objective will help guide the structure of your live stream and ensure that it's effective.

## Instagram Live: Building Personal Connections

Instagram Live is one of the most user-friendly live streaming platforms, offering features that promote interaction and visibility.

**Best Features:**

- **Live Collaborations:** Invite another user to join your live session, allowing for dual conversations that increase engagement and reach. This is perfect for interviews, collaborations, or co-hosted events.
- **Q&A and Polls:** Use Instagram's Q&A feature to collect questions from your audience ahead of time or during the stream. Polls can also be added to engage your viewers interactively.
- **Save to IGTV:** After the live stream ends, you can save the video to IGTV, ensuring that users who missed the live session can still watch it.

**Example:** A fashion blogger in New York uses Instagram Live to showcase new clothing lines in partnership with local designers. By collaborating with designers during the live stream, she expands her reach and taps into new audiences.

**Best Practices:**
- Promote your live stream in advance through stories and posts to maximize participation.

- Engage with your audience by addressing them by name and responding to their questions in real time.
- Use split-screen collaborations to boost engagement and reach new followers.

**TikTok Live: Fast-Paced and Interactive**
TikTok Live is perfect for creators who thrive in a fast-paced, high-energy environment. With TikTok's younger audience, your live sessions should be dynamic, creative, and highly engaging.

**Best Features:**
- **Gift-Giving:** Viewers can send virtual gifts during your live stream, which can be converted into monetary rewards. This feature encourages participation and creates a sense of community.
- **Moderation Tools:** TikTok allows you to designate moderators who can manage comments and keep the conversation flowing smoothly.
- **Discoverability:** TikTok promotes live streams in the "For You" page, making it easy for new users to discover your content.

**Example:** A U.S.-based artist regularly uses TikTok Live to paint in real-time, accepting requests from viewers and creating custom artwork on the spot. The interactive nature of the live stream has helped grow her audience and increase sales of her artwork.

**Best Practices:**
- Keep the energy high to match TikTok's fast-paced environment. Quick responses and playful interactions are key.
- Leverage TikTok's unique features, such as creating challenges or using popular music, to align with trending content.
- Engage with gift-givers and express appreciation in real time to foster a supportive community.

## YouTube Live: Long-Form Engagement and Monetization

YouTube Live is ideal for longer, more in-depth content. It's perfect for tutorials, interviews, and webinars. Since YouTube prioritizes video content, your live streams can also be monetized through ads, Super Chats, and channel memberships.

**Best Features:**
- **Monetization:** YouTube offers a variety of monetization options, including ads and Super Chats, where viewers pay to have their comments highlighted.
- **Replayability:** Your live stream automatically saves to your channel as a

video, giving you additional content that can continue to generate views and engagement after the live session ends.

- **Higher Production Value:** YouTube Live allows for more professional setups, including multi-camera angles and higher video quality, making it ideal for creators with more advanced production needs.

**Example:** A tech reviewer in California uses YouTube Live to host weekly product unboxings and reviews, answering questions from viewers and providing detailed insights on new gadgets. The long-form nature of the platform allows for thorough explanations and deep audience engagement.

## Best Practices:
- Plan longer sessions that allow for in-depth discussions and interaction with your audience.
- Use Super Chats to generate revenue and highlight key comments from engaged viewers.
- Invest in quality equipment to ensure your live stream is professional and visually appealing.

## Promoting Your Live Stream for Maximum Viewership

The success of your live stream often depends on how well you promote it beforehand. Use these strategies to build anticipation and ensure that your audience is ready to tune in:

- **Cross-Platform Promotion:** Use all your social media platforms to announce your live stream. For instance, promote your YouTube Live on Instagram and Facebook to attract a wider audience.
- **Teasers and Sneak Peeks:** Post teasers of what your live stream will cover, generating excitement and curiosity among your followers.
- **Scheduled Reminders:** Use countdowns and reminders on Instagram Stories or Facebook Events to keep your audience aware of the upcoming session.

**Example:** A lifestyle vlogger in Los Angeles builds anticipation for her YouTube Live Q&A by promoting it with Instagram stories and Twitter posts, ensuring that her audience is primed and ready to join the session.

## Interacting with Your Audience During a Live Stream

Interaction is the cornerstone of a successful live stream. Whether you're responding to questions, calling out viewers by name, or running live polls, these actions make your audience feel valued and engaged.

**Engagement Tactics:**
- **Live Q&A:** Encourage viewers to ask questions and answer them in real time to foster deeper interaction.
- **Polls and Surveys:** Use polls or quick surveys to gather instant feedback from your audience and make the session more interactive.
- **Shoutouts and Acknowledgments:** Personalize your live session by calling out specific viewers who participate, such as those who ask questions or send virtual gifts.

**Example:** A U.S.-based entrepreneur uses Instagram Live to host "Ask Me Anything" sessions, where viewers can submit questions about business growth. The personalized shoutouts and direct responses create an intimate and engaging atmosphere.

## Post-Live Stream Strategies: Keeping the Engagement Going

After the live stream ends, your work isn't over. Keeping the momentum going is crucial to maintaining and nurturing your audience. Here are some post-live strategies to keep your followers engaged:

- **Replay and Highlights:** Share the live stream replay on your profile or YouTube channel so that users who missed the event can still watch. Create highlights or key takeaways from the live session to repurpose into social media posts.
- **Follow-Up Content:** After the live stream, consider creating follow-up content that references or builds upon the session. For example, post a Q&A recap on Instagram or a blog summarizing key insights.
- **Audience Polls:** Ask your audience for feedback on the live stream and use their suggestions to improve future sessions.

**Example:** A food blogger in the U.S. hosts cooking demonstrations on YouTube Live, and afterward, she shares a highlights reel on Instagram with a link to the full replay on her YouTube channel. This keeps the content alive and encourages continued engagement.

### Case Study: Leveraging Live Streaming for Explosive Growth

**Case Study:** A personal development coach in the U.S. started hosting weekly Instagram Live sessions, where she offered free coaching advice and answered audience questions. By promoting the live streams on all her social media channels, she grew her Instagram followers from 5,000 to 50,000 in just six months. Her candid, real-time interaction and valuable insights helped her build a loyal community, and she was able to convert many of her live viewers into paying clients for her online courses.

Mastering live streaming is a game-changer for brands and entrepreneurs looking to build deeper, more meaningful connections with their audience. Whether you're using Instagram Live, TikTok Live, or YouTube Live, each platform offers unique opportunities to boost engagement and grow your following. By planning effectively, interacting with your audience, and leveraging each platform's features, you can turn live streaming into a powerful tool for your social media marketing strategy.

# Chapter 12

# Turning Your Followers into a Movement

In today's social media landscape, having followers isn't enough—you need to create a community that not only engages with your content but also feels connected to your mission, values, or message. The key to long-term success is inspiring action and building loyalty among your followers, transforming them from passive observers into active participants in your brand's journey.

In this chapter, we will explore how to craft content that goes beyond likes and shares, motivating your audience to take meaningful action. By tapping into your audience's emotions, values, and shared goals, you can cultivate a loyal following that feels personally invested in your brand and its success.

## From Audience to Movement: Understanding the Shift

Social media today isn't just about getting people to follow you; it's about turning those followers into a community with shared values, interests, and goals. A movement is formed when your followers feel personally connected to your message and are inspired to take action that aligns with their beliefs or desires.

**Example:** A fitness influencer in the U.S. who promotes body positivity regularly shares content that encourages followers to embrace their bodies, regardless of size or shape. Over time, she built a movement around self-love and fitness for all, leading her followers to not just watch her content but actively engage in her mission, share her message, and support her fitness programs.

**Key Elements of a Movement:**
- **Emotional Connection:** Your audience needs to feel emotionally connected to your message or mission.
- **Shared Goals:** A movement thrives when there is a collective vision or goal that followers can work toward together.
- **Action-Oriented Content:** Inspire followers to take action, whether that's participating in a challenge, sharing your message, or supporting a cause.

## Identifying What Motivates Your Audience

The first step in creating content that inspires action is understanding what motivates your audience. People are more likely to take action when they feel like they are part of something bigger than themselves.

**Questions to Ask:**
- What are your audience's core values and beliefs?
- What challenges or pain points are they facing that you can help solve?
- What are their goals and aspirations, and how can your content help them achieve those?

By identifying what truly motivates your audience, you can create content that speaks to their desires and challenges, making them feel seen and understood.

**Example:** A U.S.-based environmental activist uses social media to raise awareness about climate change. By sharing actionable steps—like reducing plastic use or participating in local cleanups—she turns her followers into active participants in her movement, empowering them to make a difference in their own communities.

## Crafting Content that Inspires Action
Inspiring action through content requires a balance of emotional storytelling, actionable steps, and clear calls to action. Your content

should motivate followers to go beyond passive engagement and take real, tangible steps in support of your message or brand.

**1. Emotional Storytelling:** Stories have the power to inspire action. Share stories that resonate with your audience's experiences, challenges, or goals. This could be your personal journey, customer testimonials, or behind-the-scenes insights into your brand.

**Example:** A U.S.-based entrepreneur shares her journey of starting a small business from her garage. By highlighting her struggles and eventual success, she encourages her followers to pursue their entrepreneurial dreams, leading to a loyal community of aspiring business owners who support her brand.

**2. Clear Calls to Action (CTAs):** Make it easy for your audience to take the next step. Whether it's joining a cause, purchasing a product, or sharing your content, provide clear, simple instructions on what to do next.

**Example:** A non-profit organization uses social media to promote fundraising campaigns. Their posts include a direct CTA: "Donate today to help us provide clean water to communities in need," followed by a link to the donation page.

**3. Shareable Content:** Content that inspires action often gets shared more widely. Create posts, videos, or infographics that are not only meaningful but also visually appealing and easy to share. This expands your reach and brings more people into your movement.

**Example:** A health advocate creates visually striking infographics that provide tips on how to eat healthier and reduce stress. These posts are shared widely on Instagram and Pinterest, increasing her follower count and solidifying her position as an authority in the wellness space.

### Building Trust Through Consistency and Authenticity

Trust is the foundation of loyalty. To turn your followers into a movement, they need to trust that your message is genuine and that you're committed to the values you promote. This trust is built through consistent, authentic content over time.

### Tips for Building Trust:
- **Be Transparent:** Share both your successes and your struggles. Followers appreciate honesty and are more likely to connect with you when they see the real, unpolished version of your journey.

- **Deliver Consistent Value:** Consistency is key. Whether it's daily tips, weekly live streams, or monthly newsletters, provide value to your audience on a regular basis.
- **Engage Authentically:** Respond to comments, messages, and questions with genuine care and attention. Authentic engagement shows that you value your audience and are invested in building a community, not just growing numbers.

**Example:** A mental health advocate on Instagram regularly shares personal stories of overcoming anxiety and depression, along with resources and tools that help her audience. Her consistent, authentic content has built a loyal following that sees her as a trusted voice in the mental health space.

## Empowering Your Audience to Take Action

One of the most effective ways to create a loyal community is by empowering your followers to take action. Empowerment comes from giving your audience the tools, resources, and motivation to make changes in their own lives.

### Action-Oriented Content Ideas:
- **Challenges:** Create social media challenges that encourage your audience to take specific

actions aligned with your message. Whether it's a fitness challenge, a sustainability challenge, or a self-care challenge, this not only engages your followers but also promotes a sense of community.

- **How-To Guides:** Share practical, actionable steps that your audience can follow to achieve their goals. Whether it's a blog post, a step-by-step video, or a downloadable guide, providing clear instructions helps empower your followers.
- **User-Generated Content:** Encourage your audience to share their own stories, successes, and experiences related to your message. This not only increases engagement but also gives your followers a sense of ownership in the movement.

**Example:** A U.S.-based fashion influencer launched a month-long "sustainable style" challenge, where followers were encouraged to wear and share outfits made from eco-friendly materials. By empowering her audience to participate and share their own content, she created a larger movement around sustainable fashion, with hundreds of followers joining in.

## The Power of Social Proof: Showcasing Success Stories

Social proof is a powerful tool for building credibility and loyalty. When people see others successfully engaging with your brand or message, they are more likely to join in themselves. Highlighting success stories from your followers can inspire others to take action and become part of your movement.

### How to Use Social Proof:

- **Share Testimonials:** Feature positive feedback, success stories, or reviews from followers who have benefited from your content or brand.
- **Highlight User-Generated Content:** Repost or share content created by your followers, whether it's testimonials, product reviews, or personal stories.
- **Showcase Achievements:** Celebrate milestones or achievements that your community has reached together, such as fundraising goals, participation numbers, or collective impact.

**Example:** A U.S.-based personal finance coach regularly shares testimonials from followers who have used her budgeting tools to pay off debt. These success stories not only validate her expertise but also inspire others to take similar steps toward financial freedom.

## Case Study: Creating a Movement Through Content

**Case Study:** A wellness influencer in the U.S. built a movement around mental health awareness by consistently sharing personal stories, helpful tips, and resources for managing anxiety and stress. She created a recurring #MindfulMonday challenge, where followers shared their own mindfulness practices. Over time, her audience grew into a community of individuals who felt empowered to prioritize their mental health. By focusing on actionable content, authentic engagement, and emotional connection, she turned her followers into a movement that continues to grow and inspire.

Building a movement is about more than just gaining followers; it's about inspiring loyalty, action, and a shared sense of purpose. By crafting content that speaks to your audience's values and empowers them to take meaningful steps, you can transform your social media presence into a powerful community-driven force.

# Part 4

# Monetizing and Scaling Your Social Media Influence

# Chapter 13

# Turning Followers into Income: Brand Deals, Sponsored Posts, and Ads

As your social media following grows, so do the opportunities to monetize your platform. From partnering with brands to creating sponsored posts and running ads, turning your followers into a source of income is a major goal for many influencers, content creators, and personal brands. In this chapter, we'll dive into the strategies and methods you can use to earn money directly from your audience by leveraging your influence.

### The Power of Social Media Influence

Social media platforms like Instagram, YouTube, TikTok, and even X (formerly Twitter) have become powerful tools for individuals to earn money through their online presence. Brands are increasingly turning to influencers and content creators to promote their products and services because followers trust the voices they engage with regularly. For

U.S.-based creators, this can mean significant income opportunities, as companies tap into influencers to reach specific audiences more authentically than traditional ads.

**Example:** A U.S.-based lifestyle blogger with 100,000 Instagram followers might make between $1,000 and $2,000 per sponsored post, depending on the brand, industry, and engagement rates. With consistent partnerships and promotions, this income stream can turn into a full-time business.

### How to Attract Brand Deals
To start earning money through brand deals, you first need to attract the right kind of attention from companies that align with your personal brand and audience. Here's how to set yourself up for success:

**1. Build a Niche and a Consistent Brand Identity:** Companies look for influencers who speak to a specific audience or have a unique voice. Whether you're focused on fitness, fashion, tech, or wellness, being clear about your niche makes you more appealing to brands.

**Example:** A U.S.-based fitness influencer who regularly posts workout routines and health tips is more likely to be approached by fitness-related brands like athletic wear companies or supplement brands than a general lifestyle account.

**2. Engagement Matters More Than Follower Count:** Brands value influencers with high engagement rates because it indicates that followers are actively paying attention to your content. Prioritize creating authentic content that resonates with your audience and encourages interaction.

**3. Reach Out to Brands:** Don't wait for brands to find you. If you have an engaged audience and content that aligns with a company's values or product, you can reach out to them directly. Pitch yourself as a collaborator and highlight how your audience matches their target market.

**Tip:** U.S.-based platforms like AspireIQ and Upfluence connect influencers with brands, making it easier to find paid partnerships.

## Sponsored Posts

### How to Create Effective Promotions
Once you've landed brand deals, the next step is creating sponsored posts that feel authentic to your audience while satisfying the brand's goals. Sponsored content should blend

seamlessly with your regular posts and offer value to your followers.

**1. Transparency and Authenticity:** Always disclose that a post is sponsored, as required by U.S. Federal Trade Commission (FTC) guidelines. Authenticity is key—your followers will appreciate honesty, and it helps maintain trust.

**Example:** If you're promoting a new skincare product on Instagram, share your personal experience with it, including why you love it, how it's helped you, and what your followers can expect if they try it.

**2. Keep the Brand's Goals in Mind:** Sponsored posts should meet the brand's objectives, whether that's increasing brand awareness, driving traffic to their website, or generating sales. Be clear about what the company wants to achieve and incorporate that into your content.

**3. Make It Engaging:** Just because a post is sponsored doesn't mean it has to feel like a commercial. Get creative! Whether through storytelling, a demo, or an unboxing video, make the content fun and engaging for your followers.

**Example:** A U.S.-based travel influencer might create an Instagram Reel showing off a sponsored luggage brand during a trip. By combining stunning travel visuals with a helpful product, they're delivering value while still promoting the brand.

### Monetizing Through Ads

In addition to brand deals and sponsored posts, running ads on platforms like YouTube, TikTok, and Instagram can bring in significant income. Here's how to optimize this revenue stream:

**1. YouTube Ad Revenue:** For creators on YouTube, joining the YouTube Partner Program (YPP) is essential for earning money through ads. Once you meet the eligibility requirements (e.g., 1,000 subscribers and 4,000 watch hours in the past 12 months), you can begin earning from ad placements on your videos.

**Example:** A U.S.-based tech reviewer who consistently posts in-depth reviews on new gadgets could earn thousands of dollars from ad revenue if they generate substantial views and high audience engagement.

**2. TikTok Creator Fund and Ads:** TikTok's Creator Fund allows eligible creators to earn money based on video performance. You can also run ads on TikTok to promote products, either through your own brand or as part of a paid collaboration with another brand.

**Example:** A U.S. beauty influencer who creates viral makeup tutorials might join the TikTok Creator Fund, earning money based on the number of views their videos receive, while also landing brand deals with cosmetics companies.

**3. Instagram Ads:** If you've transitioned to creating ads for Instagram, you can also tap into this revenue source by partnering with brands that want to run paid ads through your profile. This helps boost their reach while also offering you another income stream.

## Negotiating Rates and Deliverables

As you grow your social media following, your value to brands increases. Knowing how to negotiate your rates and deliverables is crucial for ensuring you're compensated fairly for your work. Here's what to consider:

**1. Base Your Rate on Reach and Engagement:** Rates for sponsored content and brand deals can vary widely depending on your follower count, engagement rate, and the type of content you're creating. Use industry-standard tools (like Social Bluebook) to determine a fair rate, but also account for the time and effort involved in creating high-quality content.

**Example:** For an Instagram influencer in the U.S. with around 50,000 followers, sponsored posts might range from $250 to $750 per post, depending on engagement levels and content quality.

**2. Clarify Deliverables:** Before agreeing to any brand partnership, clarify what's expected of you. This includes the number of posts, the platform they'll appear on, any specific talking points, and deadlines for content submission.

**Tip:** Have a standard contract in place that outlines the terms, including payment schedule, usage rights, and scope of work. U.S.-based influencers often rely on influencer marketing platforms like AspireIQ or direct brand contracts for this.

**Creating Long-Term Brand Partnerships**
While one-off deals can provide a nice income boost, long-term brand partnerships can offer more stability and larger paydays. Here's how to build lasting relationships with brands:

**1. Focus on Brands You Genuinely Love:** Authenticity is key to a successful long-term partnership. Work with brands that align with your personal values, style, and audience. The more natural the fit, the more likely the collaboration will be a success for both you and the brand.

**2. Deliver Consistent Value:** Show brands that you can deliver results. Consistently high engagement, quality content, and positive feedback from your followers make you more attractive for future collaborations.

**3. Pitch Retainer Deals:** Once you've established a relationship with a brand, you can pitch them on a retainer deal. This means they'll pay you a set fee each month in exchange for ongoing content, which provides both parties with greater security and consistency.

**Example:** A U.S. fitness influencer who regularly partners with a sports nutrition company might secure a six-month deal to promote their products, creating multiple posts, stories, and product placements each month.

## Case Study: Turning Followers into Full-Time Income

**Case Study:** A beauty influencer based in the U.S. started with a modest Instagram following of 10,000 people, posting makeup tutorials and product reviews. She consistently engaged with her audience, used Instagram Stories and Reels, and grew her following to over 100,000 within a year. By securing brand partnerships with major cosmetics companies, creating sponsored posts, and running affiliate marketing campaigns, she turned her hobby into a full-time job, earning more than $150,000 annually through a combination of brand deals, sponsored posts, and affiliate sales.

Monetizing your social media presence isn't just about follower count—it's about leveraging your influence to build valuable partnerships, create engaging sponsored content, and strategically use ads to generate income. By understanding how to attract brands, negotiate rates, and craft authentic content, you can turn your social media platform into a profitable business while staying true to your personal brand.

# Chapter 14

# Affiliate Marketing and Product Promotion

Affiliate marketing and product promotion are powerful ways to turn your social media presence into a revenue-generating machine. With the right strategies, you can recommend products or services to your audience and earn a commission for every sale or action they complete. This chapter will guide you through the process of maximizing your income through affiliate marketing and strategic product promotion, ensuring you monetize your influence without overwhelming your followers.

## What is Affiliate Marketing?
Affiliate marketing is a performance-based marketing strategy where you promote a product or service and earn a commission for each sale, lead, or action generated through your referral link. This model allows you to monetize your social media platforms without relying on brand sponsorships or product creation, making it an accessible and scalable income stream.

Platforms like Amazon Associates, ShareASale, and Impact Radius are widely used in the U.S. by influencers and content creators to promote products across various niches, from beauty and tech to fitness and fashion.

## How to Choose the Right Affiliate Products

The first step in successful affiliate marketing is selecting the right products to promote. Here are some tips to ensure your recommendations align with your brand and resonate with your audience:

**1. Promote Products You Actually Use:** Authenticity is crucial. Choose products that you personally use and believe in, as this builds trust with your followers. If your audience sees you genuinely benefiting from a product, they are more likely to engage with your recommendations.

**Example:** A U.S.-based beauty influencer might promote makeup or skincare products they personally use in their daily routine. This increases credibility and drives higher conversion rates.

**2. Align with Your Niche:** Stick to products that fit within your content niche. If you're a fitness influencer, promote workout gear, supplements, or health-related products. If you're a tech reviewer, focus on gadgets, software, or online courses.

**3. Research Product Reputation and Reviews:** Before promoting an affiliate product, research customer feedback and the product's reputation. Your followers trust you to recommend quality, and promoting subpar products can damage your credibility.

**4. Focus on High-Commission Products:** Many affiliate programs offer varying commission rates, from small percentages to high-ticket commissions for premium products. Balancing high-quality, high-commission products with those your audience can afford ensures better results.

### Where to Find Affiliate Programs
Finding the right affiliate programs is essential to kick-start your affiliate marketing journey. Here are some popular platforms used by U.S.-based influencers to join affiliate programs and access a wide variety of products:

**1. Amazon Associates:** As one of the largest affiliate marketing platforms, Amazon Associates allows you to promote millions of products across all categories. It's user-friendly and ideal for influencers in the U.S. because of Amazon's extensive reach.

**Example:** A lifestyle blogger might share Amazon affiliate links for home decor items featured in their Instagram posts or YouTube videos.

**2. ShareASale and Impact Radius:** These platforms connect influencers with brands that offer affiliate programs. You can apply to promote specific products or services, giving you access to a diverse range of industries.

**3. Brand-Specific Affiliate Programs:** Many brands, especially in the fashion, fitness, and tech industries, run their own affiliate programs. Research brands you love to see if they offer an affiliate program, and apply directly to become a partner.

**Example:** A U.S.-based fitness influencer could join Lululemon's affiliate program and promote their athletic wear with personalized links on their Instagram page.

### Best Practices for Promoting Affiliate Products

To maximize your revenue potential with affiliate marketing, you need to integrate your promotions seamlessly into your content. Here's how to do it effectively:

**1. Weave Affiliate Links Into Your Content:** Rather than making your affiliate promotions feel like blatant advertisements, incorporate them naturally into your posts, stories, and videos. Provide value by explaining how the product benefits you, offering tips or tutorials, and demonstrating its use.

**Example:** A tech YouTuber might create a tutorial on building a home office and seamlessly promote affiliate products like a desk, chair, and accessories, with links in the video description.

**2. Use Multiple Platforms:** Don't limit yourself to just one platform. Promote affiliate links on Instagram, YouTube, TikTok, Facebook, or your personal blog. Each platform offers unique opportunities to reach different segments of your audience.

**Tip:** Instagram Stories, with their "Swipe Up" feature, or TikTok bio links are great for driving traffic to affiliate products quickly.

**3. Create Dedicated Content:** In addition to integrating affiliate links into your regular posts, consider creating dedicated content around a specific product. This could be a full review, a tutorial, or a "best of" list where you feature several related affiliate products.

**Example:** A fashion blogger might create a "Fall Wardrobe Essentials" blog post featuring affiliate links to their favorite outfits.

**4. Transparency and Disclosure:** Always be transparent about your affiliate partnerships. The U.S. Federal Trade Commission (FTC) requires influencers to disclose when they are using affiliate links. Being upfront about affiliate promotions builds trust and ensures compliance with legal requirements.

**Tip:** Use phrases like "I may earn a small commission if you make a purchase through these links" to clarify that the post contains affiliate links.

## Maximizing Affiliate Marketing on Different Platforms

Each social media platform offers unique opportunities for affiliate marketing. Here's how to tailor your strategy based on the platform:

**1. Instagram:** Instagram Stories, Reels, and IGTV videos are great for showcasing affiliate products. Use Instagram's native shopping features or include affiliate links in your bio. Make sure to provide clear calls to action, such as "Swipe Up" or "Link in Bio," to direct followers to your affiliate products.

**2. YouTube:** YouTube is perfect for product reviews, tutorials, and unboxings. Include affiliate links in the video description, and mention the links verbally during the video. Long-form content allows you to dive deep into product features and benefits.

**Example:** A tech reviewer might include affiliate links to all the gear and software used in their videos, encouraging viewers to purchase via the links.

**3. TikTok:** TikTok's short-form videos allow you to get creative with product demos or quick tutorials. Place affiliate links in your bio and direct viewers to check them out. TikTok's massive reach and viral potential make it a powerful platform for affiliate marketing.

**4. Blogging and Email Marketing:** If you have a personal blog or email newsletter, these are also prime spaces for affiliate marketing. Write product reviews, comparison articles, or "how-to" guides that incorporate affiliate links, and send them directly to your audience's inbox.

## The Art of Product Promotion: Creating Content that Converts

Creating content that drives affiliate sales requires a thoughtful approach to product promotion. Here's how to turn your posts into conversion machines:

**1. Focus on Benefits, Not Features:** Rather than just listing features of the product, focus on how it solves a problem or enhances your followers' lives. People are more likely to purchase something if they see how it directly benefits them.

**Example:** If promoting a new laptop, talk about how it speeds up your workflow and makes it easier to manage your daily tasks, rather than just listing technical specifications.

**2. Create Urgency:** Limited-time offers or seasonal promotions can drive urgency and push your audience to take action. Mention sales, discounts, or exclusive offers tied to your affiliate links to increase conversions.

**3. Show, Don't Just Tell:** Visual storytelling is key. Instead of merely talking about the product, show your audience how it works in real-time. Use videos, before-and-after shots, or tutorials to visually demonstrate the product's value.

**Example:** A fitness influencer promoting a workout supplement might create a TikTok showing their fitness routine and results, encouraging followers to try the supplement through an affiliate link.

### Measuring and Tracking Success

To maximize your affiliate marketing efforts, it's important to track your results and optimize your strategy. Here's how to measure success:

**1. Use Analytics Tools:** Most affiliate platforms, including Amazon Associates and ShareASale, provide detailed analytics on clicks, conversions, and earnings. Monitor these metrics to understand which products resonate most with your audience.

**2. A/B Testing:** Try different approaches to see what works best. Experiment with various types of content, product placement, and calls to action to see what generates the most affiliate sales.

**3. Optimize Your Links:** Use UTM parameters to track where your clicks are coming from. This way, you can see whether your affiliate links perform better on Instagram, YouTube, or TikTok and adjust your strategy accordingly.

## Case Study: Affiliate Marketing Success Story

**Case Study:** A fashion blogger based in the U.S. started promoting Amazon fashion finds through their Instagram Stories and blog. By focusing on affordable yet stylish pieces, they built a loyal audience that trusted their recommendations. Over time, their affiliate sales grew from a few hundred dollars a month to over $10,000 per month during major shopping events like Black Friday and Cyber Monday, all through carefully curated content and consistent affiliate marketing efforts.

Affiliate marketing and product promotion are powerful ways to monetize your social media presence without the need for constant brand deals or creating your own products. By selecting the right affiliate products, weaving promotions naturally into your content, and strategically leveraging each platform's unique features, you can maximize your revenue potential while maintaining an authentic connection with your audience.

# Chapter 15

# Building and Selling Your Own Products or Services

Building and selling your own products or services on social media is one of the most rewarding ways to monetize your online presence. Whether you want to create a digital course, launch branded merchandise, or offer specialized services, leveraging your social media following gives you a direct line to potential customers. In this chapter, we'll walk you through the process of transforming your ideas into real products and services that resonate with your audience and generate sustainable income.

## The Power of Owning Your Own Product

Owning your own product or service allows you to take control of your income and brand identity. Unlike affiliate marketing or sponsored posts, where you rely on external products and companies, creating your own offerings gives you full control over what you deliver and how you market it.

**Why It Matters:**

- **Greater Profit Margins:** You keep all of the profit from sales, instead of earning a percentage from a third party.
- **Creative Freedom:** You can tailor your product or service to the exact needs of your audience.
- **Long-Term Sustainability:** Building a product that reflects your expertise can position you as an authority in your niche.

### Identifying the Right Product or Service for Your Brand

Before diving into product creation, it's crucial to identify what kind of product or service would best suit your personal brand and resonate with your audience. Here's how to do that:

**1. Know Your Audience's Needs:** The most successful products are those that solve a problem or fulfill a need for your audience. Use social media insights, direct feedback, and engagement metrics to understand what your followers are asking for.

**Example:** If you're a fitness influencer in the U.S. and receive constant questions about workout plans, consider creating a digital fitness program tailored to beginner or advanced users.

**2. Choose a Product That Aligns with Your Expertise:** Stick to what you know. If you've built your social media presence around beauty tips, creating a skincare line or beauty course makes more sense than venturing into a completely unrelated field.

**3. Evaluate Demand and Competition:** Look at similar products or services already available in your niche. Conduct research to find gaps in the market or ways to differentiate your offering. Standing out with unique value propositions—whether it's a specialized course, one-on-one services, or custom merch—can help you attract a loyal audience.

### Types of Products You Can Offer

Here are the most popular types of products and services you can build to sell on social media:

**1. Digital Courses and eBooks:** Monetize your expertise by creating educational content in the form of online courses, eBooks, or guides. Platforms like Teachable, Udemy, and Gumroad allow you to host and sell your content easily.

**Example:** A social media strategist might create a digital course on "Growing Your TikTok Followers from 0 to 100k in 6 Months."

**2. Physical Products and Merch:** For those with a large, dedicated following, selling physical products like clothing, mugs, or branded merchandise can be a great way to monetize your influence. Platforms like Printful and Teespring allow you to create and sell custom products without upfront inventory costs.

**Example:** A U.S.-based artist might sell custom-designed t-shirts or posters featuring their artwork through an online store.

**3. Subscription Services or Memberships:** Offer exclusive content, behind-the-scenes access, or direct communication through paid memberships on platforms like Patreon or through private Facebook groups. Subscriptions create a steady stream of recurring income and deepen engagement with your most dedicated fans.

**Example:** A business coach could create a members-only group offering weekly coaching sessions, webinars, and resources.

**4. Consulting or Coaching Services:** Offer personalized consulting or coaching sessions for individuals or businesses looking for tailored advice in your area of expertise. Whether it's social media marketing, fitness training, or career coaching, direct one-on-one services can command higher fees and build deeper client relationships.

**Example:** A personal finance influencer might offer consulting sessions to help people create personalized savings plans or investment strategies.

## The Step-by-Step Guide to Product Creation

Once you've identified the right product or service, it's time to bring it to life. Here's a step-by-step guide to developing and launching your product:

**Step 1: Validate Your Idea** Before investing time and resources, validate your product idea by asking your audience for feedback. Use polls, surveys, or beta tests to gauge interest and refine your concept based on their input.

**Tip:** Platforms like Instagram Stories allow you to use polls or questions to quickly gather feedback on product ideas.

**Step 2: Develop Your Product** Create your product or service with your audience's needs in mind. If you're creating a digital course, outline the lessons, shoot video content, and create any accompanying materials. If you're offering merchandise, design the product and source quality manufacturers.

**Step 3: Set Up a Sales Funnel** A well-crafted sales funnel guides potential customers from awareness to purchase. Build a landing page or online store where people can learn about your product, see its value, and make a purchase. Popular platforms include Shopify, Gumroad, or ClickFunnels.

**Example:** An online store for your merch might have a simple homepage featuring bestsellers, customer reviews, and an easy checkout process.

**Step 4: Price Your Product Strategically** Pricing can make or break the success of your product. Consider your target audience's budget and the value you're offering. High-ticket items like coaching or digital courses may require more in-depth sales efforts, while low-cost items like eBooks can sell in higher volumes.

**Step 5: Promote Your Product on Social Media** Use your existing social media presence to promote your product through organic posts, Stories, Reels, and live videos. Create excitement by announcing the product launch, showing behind-the-scenes content, and offering limited-time discounts or bonuses.

**Best Platforms for Selling Your Products**
Depending on the type of product or service you create, different platforms may be best suited for your business. Here are some popular options:

**1. Shopify for E-commerce:** Shopify is ideal for selling physical products or merch, with features that allow you to create a custom online store and manage everything from shipping to inventory.

**2. Gumroad for Digital Products:** Gumroad allows you to easily sell digital products like eBooks, courses, or memberships. It's especially popular for creatives like writers, designers, and content creators.

**3. Teachable or Udemy for Online Courses:** If you're creating an online course, platforms like Teachable or Udemy allow you to host your course, track sales, and engage with students through a professional-looking platform.

**4. Patreon for Memberships:** Patreon is a subscription-based platform where you can offer exclusive content to your followers in exchange for a monthly fee. It's great for building a community and offering recurring value.

**5. Print-on-Demand Services (Printful, Teespring):** For influencers looking to create and sell custom merchandise, print-on-demand services like Printful or Teespring are perfect. They handle production and shipping, so you can focus on designing and promoting.

## Marketing and Selling Your Products to a U.S. Audience

Here are some specific strategies to reach and resonate with U.S.-based customers:

**1. Use U.S.-based Trends and Cultural References:** Leverage U.S.-specific trends, holidays, and cultural moments to connect with your audience. For example, launching a product during Black Friday, the Super Bowl, or back-to-school season can boost sales and make your product feel more relevant.

**2. Influencer Partnerships and Collaborations:** Work with other U.S.-based influencers to promote your product. Collaborating with creators who have a similar audience allows you to reach new customers while benefiting from the trust they've built with their followers.

**Example:** A beauty influencer might collaborate with another influencer to cross-promote each other's new skincare lines.

**3. Paid Ads Targeting U.S. Markets:** Utilize social media ads on platforms like Instagram, Facebook, and TikTok to reach U.S. audiences. You can target specific demographics, interests, and locations to get your product in front of the right customers.

### Success Stories: Turning Influence into Income

**Case Study: Building a Six-Figure Digital Course** A U.S.-based fitness influencer with a large Instagram following created a digital course titled "30 Days to Your Best Body" featuring workout plans, nutrition guides, and video demonstrations. By using Instagram Stories to showcase client success stories and offering early-bird discounts to their most engaged followers, they successfully launched the course, earning six figures within the first six months.

Creating and selling your own products or services on social media is one of the most effective ways to monetize your following and build a long-term, sustainable income stream. Whether it's digital courses, merchandise, or consulting services, the key is to stay authentic, cater to your audience's needs, and provide real value. By leveraging the power of your social media presence, you can turn your influence into a thriving business.

# Part 5

# Tracking Progress and Staying Consistent

# Chapter 16

# Social Media Analytics

To grow your social media presence and achieve viral success, it's essential to track and analyze your performance. Social media analytics help you understand what's working, what isn't, and how to improve. Mastering key metrics and tools, while staying ahead of ever-changing algorithms, will give you the edge needed to keep growing your followers and influence.

**Why Social Media Analytics Matter**
Analytics are the backbone of a successful social media strategy. They provide data-driven insights into how your content is performing, who your audience is, and what tactics drive engagement. By paying attention to analytics, you can:

- **Identify What Resonates with Your Audience:** Find out which posts, stories, or videos get the most likes, shares, and comments to replicate their success.
- **Refine Your Content Strategy:** Analytics help you see which content types (e.g., videos, photos, infographics) perform best, so you can focus on what works.

- **Measure ROI (Return on Investment):** If you're investing time or money in social media (e.g., ads, collaborations), analytics help ensure you're getting value from your efforts.
- **Understand Algorithmic Impact:** Algorithms prioritize content based on various factors. Analytics help you adapt to these changes by showing you what's getting pushed forward or hidden from your audience.

## Key Metrics to Track for Social Media Success

Different platforms have varying metrics, but certain key performance indicators (KPIs) are universally important. Here are the essential metrics to focus on for growth:

### 1. Engagement Rate

This includes likes, comments, shares, retweets, and saves. High engagement is a sign that your content is resonating with your audience. Engagement rate is often more valuable than follower count because it shows how active and connected your audience is.

**How to Calculate Engagement Rate:** Divide the total number of engagements (likes, comments, shares, etc.) by your total followers, then multiply by 100.

## 2. Reach and Impressions

- **Reach** refers to how many unique users saw your content. It gives you an idea of how wide your audience is.
- **Impressions** are the total number of times your content was displayed, even if the same user saw it multiple times. This helps you gauge how visible your content is on a platform.

## 3. Follower Growth Rate

This measures how fast your follower count is increasing over time. It's not just about how many followers you have, but how quickly you're growing. A steady growth rate indicates that your content is consistently attracting new people.

## 4. Click-Through Rate (CTR)

CTR measures how often people who see your posts click on a link in your bio, swipe up in Stories, or engage with a call-to-action (CTA). It's crucial for campaigns that drive traffic to external sites like blogs, product pages, or affiliate links.

**How to Calculate CTR:** Divide the number of clicks by the total number of impressions or views, then multiply by 100.

## 5. Conversion Rate

Conversion rate shows how many people take a desired action after interacting with your social media content. This could be signing up for a newsletter, purchasing a product, or downloading a resource. It's particularly important for monetizing your presence.

### Best Tools for Social Media Analytics

Several tools make it easier to gather and interpret social media data. Here are some of the best platforms for tracking analytics across different social media networks:

### 1. Native Analytics Tools

Most social platforms offer built-in analytics tools that give you direct insights into your performance.

- **Instagram Insights:** Provides data on engagement, reach, impressions, and follower demographics.
- **Facebook Insights:** Offers page-level data like likes, post reach, and engagement.
- **YouTube Analytics:** Gives detailed metrics on watch time, audience retention, and traffic sources.
- **TikTok Analytics:** Tracks follower growth, video views, and engagement rates.

## 2. Google Analytics

While Google Analytics is generally used for websites, it can also be helpful for tracking social media referrals, traffic, and conversions. You can track how much of your website traffic comes from different social media platforms.

## 3. Hootsuite Analytics

Hootsuite is a social media management tool that consolidates data from multiple platforms. It provides insights into audience behavior, engagement trends, and the best times to post.

## 4. Sprout Social

Sprout Social offers comprehensive reports across several platforms, including Instagram, Facebook, Twitter (X), and LinkedIn. Its reporting tools break down audience demographics, engagement trends, and even social listening (what people are saying about your brand).

## 5. Later

Later is great for Instagram users, providing detailed data on your post performance, including best times to post and hashtag effectiveness.

## 6. BuzzSumo

BuzzSumo is excellent for tracking the performance of your content across social networks, especially for identifying viral trends and high-performing posts within your niche.

## Adapting to Social Media Algorithm Changes

One of the biggest challenges in social media growth is keeping up with constant algorithm changes. These algorithms determine who sees your content and how often it's shown, making it vital to stay adaptable.

### 1. How Algorithms Work

Each platform has its own algorithm that ranks content based on various factors, such as:

- **Engagement Levels:** The more likes, shares, and comments a post gets in a short amount of time, the more likely it is to be shown to a wider audience.
- **Relevancy and Interests:** Algorithms use data on what users interact with to prioritize content that aligns with their interests.
- **Recency:** Most algorithms favor fresh content, so consistent posting is essential.
- **Platform-Specific Priorities:** For example, TikTok's algorithm prioritizes content discovery, pushing viral videos to new users, while Instagram prioritizes engagement within your existing follower base.

**2. Staying Ahead of Changes**
Adapting to algorithm changes requires agility and awareness of trends. Here are some tips to stay ahead:

- **Follow Platform Updates:** Social media companies frequently update their algorithms. Follow blogs, official updates, and industry news to stay in the know.
- **Test and Experiment:** If you notice a dip in reach or engagement, experiment with different content formats, posting times, and strategies. Platforms like Instagram and TikTok reward users who try new things like Reels or viral challenges.
- **Engage with Followers Quickly:** Since algorithms favor engagement, responding to comments and interacting with your audience promptly can boost your content's visibility.
- **Prioritize Video Content:** Platforms like Instagram, Facebook, and TikTok are increasingly favoring video formats. Incorporating videos into your strategy—whether it's Reels, TikTok trends, or YouTube Shorts—can help you stay relevant.

### 3. Capitalizing on Algorithm Changes

Sometimes, algorithm changes can present new opportunities. For instance, Instagram's shift towards promoting Reels has opened doors for accounts to rapidly grow their reach by prioritizing short, engaging videos. Similarly, YouTube's focus on Shorts has provided new creators with greater exposure.

By staying proactive and experimenting with new features as they are released, you can use these shifts to your advantage.

## US-Based Case Study: Adapting to Algorithm Shifts

### Case Study: TikTok Influencer's Rapid Growth Amid Algorithm Changes

In early 2023, a U.S.-based fashion influencer saw a drop in engagement when TikTok adjusted its algorithm to focus more on discovery and less on following. To adapt, she began using trending music, hashtags, and challenges. Within months, her videos started landing on TikTok's "For You" page, leading to an influx of followers. By using TikTok's analytics tools to track which trends were gaining the most traction, she gained over 200,000 new followers in just six months.

## Using Analytics to Pivot and Grow

Even with algorithm changes and shifting trends, analytics give you the data you need to pivot your strategy. If you notice a particular post type or video isn't performing as well as it used to, don't be afraid to switch things up.

- **Example:** If long-form Instagram captions are not getting as much engagement, experiment with short, snappy captions or video-based content to see how your audience responds.
- **Experiment with Hashtags:** Analytics can show which hashtags bring in the most reach and which ones fall flat. Use this data to refine your hashtag strategy.

In the ever-evolving world of social media, analytics are your compass. By paying close attention to key metrics and adapting to algorithm changes, you'll ensure that your content not only reaches the right people but also resonates deeply. Mastering social media analytics is the key to staying ahead of the curve, growing your audience, and ensuring your content goes viral.

By consistently tracking performance, experimenting with new trends, and staying adaptable, you can continually refine your approach and position yourself for long-term growth.

# Chapter 17

# Consistency is Key: How to Build a Content Calendar for Long-Term Growth and Engagement

Consistency is one of the most critical factors in growing and maintaining an engaged social media audience. Successful social media influencers, brands, and creators don't rely on occasional viral posts; they grow through regular, strategic content planning. Building a content calendar ensures you stay organized, consistently deliver value to your followers, and remain aligned with your long-term goals.

## Why Consistency Matters in Social Media Growth

In social media, consistency creates familiarity, trust, and anticipation. When your audience knows you post regularly, they're more likely to return for your content, engage with it, and share it with others. Inconsistent posting, on the other hand, can lead to audience disengagement, making it harder to build a loyal following.

Here's why consistency is essential:

- **Building Trust:** Posting regularly signals that you're reliable, making your audience more likely to follow you closely and engage.
- **Staying Top-of-Mind:** In the fast-paced world of social media, regularly posting ensures you don't get lost in the noise. It keeps you visible to your audience and algorithms.
- **Strengthening the Algorithm:** Social media platforms favor accounts that consistently post quality content, rewarding them with higher visibility.
- **Enhancing Engagement:** Consistency helps you establish a rhythm for interaction, leading to stronger connections and deeper engagement with your community.

### What is a Content Calendar?

A content calendar is a strategic tool used to organize, schedule, and plan your social media posts over a set period of time (daily, weekly, monthly). It helps you maintain a steady posting schedule, plan ahead for major campaigns or events, and ensure your content aligns with your overall goals.

Key components of a content calendar:
- **Date and Time of Post:** When each post will go live.
- **Content Type:** Whether it's a video, image, blog post, meme, or infographic.
- **Platform:** Which social media platform the content will be posted on (Instagram, TikTok, YouTube, X, etc.).
- **Theme/Message:** What the core message of the post will be (e.g., education, entertainment, promotion).
- **Hashtags and Keywords:** Relevant tags or keywords to enhance visibility.
- **Call-to-Action (CTA):** The action you want your audience to take (e.g., comment, share, sign up, purchase).

## How to Build an Effective Content Calendar

Creating a content calendar that aligns with your long-term growth strategy takes careful planning and research. Here's a step-by-step guide to building one that works for you:

### 1. Define Your Social Media Goals

Your content should be driven by the goals you want to achieve. These might include:

- Growing your follower count

- Boosting engagement (likes, comments, shares)
- Driving traffic to a website, blog, or store
- Generating leads or sales
- Establishing yourself as an authority in your niche

Knowing your goals helps you focus your content creation and ensures that every post serves a purpose.

## 2. Understand Your Audience
To create content that resonates, you need to understand your target audience's interests, habits, and online behaviors. Dive into your analytics and audience insights to identify:

- **Who they are:** Demographics like age, gender, location, and interests.
- **What they engage with:** Content formats (videos, stories, memes) and topics that spark their attention.
- **When they're online:** Best times and days to post for maximum engagement.

## 3. Choose Your Platforms Wisely
Each social media platform has its unique culture, audience, and content formats. The way you approach Instagram differs from how you use TikTok or LinkedIn. Your content

calendar should reflect the nuances of each platform:

- **Instagram:** Visual storytelling through posts, Reels, and stories.
- **TikTok:** Short-form, viral content that's trend-driven.
- **YouTube:** Long-form videos for education or entertainment.
- **X (Twitter):** Real-time engagement with short, impactful messages.
- **LinkedIn:** Professional, educational content aimed at building authority.

## 4. Plan Your Content Mix

To keep your feed diverse and engaging, vary your content types. A balanced content mix might include:

- **Educational Posts:** Teach your audience something new, share tips or how-tos.
- **Entertaining Content:** Memes, challenges, or light-hearted content that's shareable.
- **Promotional Posts:** Showcase products, services, or collaborations.
- **Personal Stories:** Share behind-the-scenes moments or personal insights to build a deeper connection.

- **Engagement-Driven Posts:** Ask questions, run polls, or host giveaways to spark interaction.

## 5. Set a Posting Frequency
Decide how often you'll post on each platform. For example, you might post daily on Instagram but only once a week on YouTube. The key is to stay consistent with your schedule. If daily posting feels overwhelming, start with 3-4 posts per week and gradually increase your frequency as you streamline your process.

## 6. Use Scheduling Tools
There are several tools available that make scheduling and managing your content easier:

- **Hootsuite:** Schedule posts across multiple platforms from one dashboard.
- **Buffer:** A simple and intuitive tool for managing social media accounts.
- **Later:** A great tool for planning and scheduling Instagram posts, Reels, and stories.
- **ContentCal:** A collaborative content calendar platform perfect for teams.
- **Trello:** A project management tool that can be used as a content calendar to organize and schedule your social posts.

Scheduling your posts in advance saves time and ensures you stick to your posting schedule even during busy times.

## Content Calendar Template Example

Here's an example of how your weekly content calendar might look:

| Date | Platform | Content Type | Post Description | Hashtags | CTA |
|------|----------|--------------|------------------|----------|-----|
| Mon | Instagram | Reel | "Behind the scenes of my morning routine" | #Morning Vibes #Productivity | Share your routine in the comments |
| Tue | TikTok | Short video | "Top 5 tips for going viral on TikTok" | #ViralTips #TikTokGrowth | Follow for more tips |
| Wed | X (Twitter) | Tweet | "Quick tip: Engagement > Follower count" | #SocialMediaTips #GrowthHacks | Retweet if you agree |
| Thur | Instagram Stories | Poll | "What type of content do you want to see next?" | #InstagramPoll #ContentCreation | Vote now |
| Fri | YouTube | Long-form video | "How I grew my Instagram from 0 to 100K in 6 months" | #YouTubeGrowth #InstagramSuccess | Subscribe for more growth tips |
| Sat | LinkedIn | Article | "How to build a personal brand on social media" | #PersonalBranding #LinkedInTips | Comment your thoughts |

163

| Sun | TikTok | Viral trend | "Participating in the latest TikTok challenge" | #Trending Challenge #ForYou | Try this challenge yourself! |
| --- | --- | --- | --- | --- | --- |

This schedule shows a balanced mix of educational, personal, and engagement-driven posts that cater to different platforms.

## US-Based Case Study: A YouTuber's Content Calendar Strategy

### Case Study: From Consistent Posting to YouTube Success

In 2022, a fitness YouTuber from the U.S. found her audience was growing steadily, but not at the viral pace she desired. After analyzing her posting schedule, she realized she wasn't consistent in delivering content, which affected her algorithmic ranking. She decided to build a content calendar and commit to posting three videos a week—one long-form workout routine, one Q&A session, and one short-form video.

By planning ahead and sticking to this schedule, her subscriber count doubled within six months. Her YouTube analytics showed that consistent posting boosted her engagement and visibility, leading to more shares, comments, and recommendations from the platform's algorithm.

## Staying Consistent: Overcoming Common Challenges

Even with a content calendar, it can be difficult to stay consistent. Here are some tips to help overcome common obstacles:

- **Batch Content Creation:** Instead of creating content day-by-day, spend one day each week batching multiple pieces of content. This ensures you always have material ready to post.
- **Use Templates:** Design templates for posts, stories, and videos to streamline the creative process.
- **Repurpose Content:** Don't be afraid to reuse or repurpose content across different platforms. For example, turn a TikTok video into an Instagram Reel or use a blog post as the foundation for a LinkedIn article.
- **Stay Flexible:** While consistency is key, it's also important to stay flexible. Be ready to pivot your content calendar when new trends, events, or opportunities arise.

A well-planned content calendar is one of the most powerful tools for social media growth. It allows you to stay organized, post consistently, and track your progress toward long-term goals. By maintaining a steady flow of engaging, high-quality content, you'll not only grow your following but also create meaningful connections that drive engagement and loyalty.

The path to social media success is a marathon, not a sprint. By using a content calendar to stay consistent and intentional with your posting, you set yourself up for sustainable growth and lasting influence.

# Chapter 18

# Putting it All Together: Your Blueprint for Social Media Growth, Virality, and Success

At this stage, you've learned how to create a strong social media foundation, build an engaged audience, craft content that grabs attention, and leverage the power of various platforms. Now it's time to bring everything together and design a comprehensive blueprint that will guide your social media growth, help you go viral, and achieve lasting success.

## Recap: Key Elements of Social Media Growth

To create a successful social media strategy, you need to focus on the following key elements:

### 1. Crafting Standout Profiles and Branding

Your profile is the first thing people see. It needs to reflect your personal brand, communicate your value, and be visually appealing to draw people in. Every aspect of your profile, from your bio to your profile picture, plays a crucial role in shaping how people perceive your presence.

## 2. Identifying and Engaging Your Ideal Audience

You can't be everything to everyone. Success on social media requires you to find your specific niche or "tribe." Identifying your ideal audience helps you create tailored content that resonates, solves problems, and sparks genuine engagement.

## 3. Creating Viral-Worthy Content

Content is king. Whether it's a blog post, a TikTok video, or a meme, the key to going viral is creating content that resonates, entertains, and adds value to your audience's life. Consistently delivering attention-grabbing content is the foundation of your social media strategy.

## 4. Using Visual and Video Storytelling for Maximum Impact

Visuals are powerful. From Instagram photos to viral TikToks and YouTube videos, mastering the art of visual storytelling can exponentially grow your influence. Memes, photos, short-form videos, and well-designed graphics make your content shareable and memorable.

## 5. Growing Across Multiple Platforms

Instagram, TikTok, YouTube, Facebook, LinkedIn, and X (Twitter) all have unique audiences and content formats. By mastering each platform's strengths and adapting your content, you can increase your reach and create growth across various social media channels.

## 6. Building an Engaged Community

Followers are good, but superfans are better. A loyal community of engaged followers who interact with your posts, share your content, and support your brand is key to sustained social media success. Engagement strategies such as giveaways, live streams, and personal interaction help build this community.

## Creating Your Personalized Blueprint for Social Media Success

While the steps to social media growth may be universal, how you apply them depends on your goals, audience, and unique brand. Here's a simple blueprint to follow:

## Step 1: Set Clear Goals

Without clear goals, it's hard to measure success. Are you looking to build a large following? Create viral content? Monetize through brand deals or your own products? Your goals should guide everything from the type of content you create to how you engage with your audience.

## Example Goals:

- Reach 100,000 followers in 6 months.
- Go viral with at least one video per month.

- Generate $5,000 per month in brand deals or product sales.

## Step 2: Choose Your Primary Platforms

While it's tempting to be on every social media platform, focusing on 2-3 main platforms allows you to direct your energy and efforts for maximum impact.

### For example:

- If your goal is virality, TikTok and Instagram Reels are the best platforms for short-form video content.
- For long-form content and in-depth engagement, YouTube and LinkedIn are ideal.
- To stay connected in real-time and share thoughts quickly, X (Twitter) is a powerful tool.

## Step 3: Build a Consistent Content Strategy

Consistency is the backbone of growth. Set a realistic posting schedule and stick to it. A content calendar, as discussed in Chapter 17, will help you maintain a steady flow of posts across all platforms.

**Content Strategy Breakdown:**
- Daily: Short posts or videos (Instagram Stories, TikTok clips, Tweets)
- Weekly: In-depth posts (YouTube videos, long Instagram captions, blog posts)
- Monthly: Special campaigns (Giveaways, contests, collaborations)

## Step 4: Create High-Value, Shareable Content

Make sure your content solves a problem, entertains, or teaches something valuable. Use eye-catching visuals, creative storytelling, and concise messaging to increase your chances of going viral.

**Content Examples:**
- **TikTok:** Trending challenges, fun how-tos, or quirky viral moments.
- **Instagram:** Beautifully curated photos, motivational Reels, or behind-the-scenes content.
- **YouTube:** Informative long-form videos, tutorials, or vlogs that connect with your audience.

## Step 5: Engage, Engage, Engage

Engagement isn't just about likes and shares; it's about creating conversations. Respond to comments, interact with followers, and encourage your audience to engage with your content. The more interaction, the more likely social media algorithms will boost your posts.

### Engagement Strategies:
- Respond to every comment within the first hour of posting.
- Use polls and Q&A features on Instagram Stories.
- Host a TikTok Live or Instagram Live once a week to connect with your followers in real time.

### Step 6: Analyze and Adapt
Regularly track your performance. Use social media analytics tools to monitor your growth, engagement rates, and which types of content perform best. As social media platforms change, so should your strategy.

### Key Metrics to Monitor:
- **Follower Growth:** How fast is your audience growing?
- **Engagement Rate:** What percentage of your followers are interacting with your content?
- **Reach and Impressions:** How many people are seeing your posts?
- **Virality:** How often is your content being shared, and by whom?

**US-Based Case Study: The Rise of Charli D'Amelio on TikTok**

Charli D'Amelio, an American dancer and social media personality, rose to fame on TikTok within just a few months by consistently posting short, dance-related videos that aligned with the platform's trends. Her quick rise to TikTok fame came from her ability to:

- **Identify her niche** in dance videos.
- **Follow trends** and create her own viral dance challenges.
- **Engage with her audience** through comments and collaborations.
- **Consistently post** multiple videos a day, capitalizing on TikTok's algorithm favoring active creators.

Charli's success shows the power of consistent, viral content combined with active engagement. She's now one of the most followed TikTokers globally, with brand deals, sponsorships, and a loyal fanbase that extends beyond the app.

**Key Takeaways for Success**

As you implement this blueprint, keep these essential takeaways in mind:

- **Consistency is your greatest asset.** Showing up regularly builds trust and keeps you top-of-mind for your audience.

- **Authenticity wins.** The more real and relatable you are, the more likely people will connect with you and your content.
- **Engagement fuels growth.** Engage meaningfully with your audience to build lasting relationships and loyalty.
- **Stay adaptable.** Social media platforms and trends evolve constantly. Be ready to shift your strategy to stay relevant.
- **Quality trumps quantity.** Posting consistently doesn't mean sacrificing quality. Always aim to create valuable, shareable content.

### Your Social Media Growth Action Plan

Here's your actionable plan for immediate growth:

**1. Audit Your Profiles:** Ensure your profiles and bios are clear, optimized, and reflect your brand.

**2. Set Your Goals:** Define measurable goals for the next 3, 6, and 12 months.

**3. Select Your Platforms:** Choose 2-3 platforms where your target audience is most active.

**4. Build a Content Calendar:** Plan your posting schedule for the next 30 days, including diverse content types.

**5. Engage Your Audience:** Set aside time daily to respond to comments, DMs, and engage with followers.

**6. Analyze and Adjust:** Track your progress regularly, adapting your content based on analytics and platform changes.

With this blueprint in hand, you now have everything you need to grow your social media presence, create viral content, and build a loyal, engaged community. Remember, success on social media isn't about overnight virality—it's about consistency, creativity, and authentic connections.

By staying focused, learning from your audience, and adapting to the ever-changing world of social media, you're on your way to becoming a social media powerhouse. The journey may be long, but with persistence and a solid strategy, your social media success is within reach.

Now it's time to take action—start building your influence, connecting with your audience, and achieving the success you've always dreamed of!

# Bonus Chapter

# Staying Ahead of Social Media Trends

The world of social media is fast-paced and constantly evolving. New platforms emerge, algorithms shift, and trends that were once viral can quickly fade. To maintain a successful and sustainable social media presence, it's crucial to stay ahead of these changes and future-proof your strategy.

In this chapter, we'll explore how you can keep your finger on the pulse of social media trends, adapt to new technologies, and ensure that your strategy is flexible enough to withstand the test of time.

## Why Staying Ahead of Trends Matters

Social media is a crowded space, and the competition for attention is fierce. One of the best ways to stand out is by being ahead of the curve. Whether it's adopting a new platform early, mastering the latest feature, or creating content that taps into trending topics, staying ahead of trends allows you to:

- Gain visibility before others catch on.
- Position yourself as an innovator and thought leader.
- Take advantage of new features and algorithms designed to promote early adopters.
- Build a future-ready brand that adapts to changes in audience behavior.

## How to Spot Emerging Trends

The key to staying ahead is to develop a system for recognizing emerging trends before they become mainstream. Here are some effective ways to do that:

### 1. Follow Industry Leaders and Trendsetters

Leading influencers, marketers, and social media experts are often the first to adopt new trends. By following them on social platforms and reading their blogs or newsletters, you can gain insight into what's coming next.

### Who to follow:

- Influential creators in your niche (e.g., Gary Vaynerchuk for marketing, or Charli D'Amelio for TikTok).
- Social media-focused blogs like Social Media Examiner, Hootsuite Blog, and Sprout Social.

- Trend analysis platforms such as Exploding Topics or Google Trends.

## 2. Keep an Eye on New Platforms and Features

Platforms like TikTok started small but quickly became massive players in the social media landscape. Be open to experimenting with new platforms or features before they're widely adopted. Keep an eye out for beta releases, new app launches, or updates on established platforms (e.g., Instagram Reels or YouTube Shorts).

**Tip:** Join online communities such as Reddit's **r/socialmedia** or Facebook groups where marketers and creators share insights on new features.

## 3. Monitor Algorithm Changes

Each platform's algorithm plays a huge role in determining who sees your content. Regularly reviewing updates to algorithms will help you adjust your content strategy to maintain visibility and engagement.

### Tools for tracking algorithm changes:
- Later Blog for Instagram updates.
- Search Engine Journal and Moz Blog for broader algorithm news.
- The Verge for platform feature updates.

### 4. Leverage Data and Analytics

Your own social media analytics can reveal trends in how your audience is interacting with your content. Are videos performing better than images? Are engagement rates higher on certain platforms? Use this data to adjust your strategy to match what your audience wants.

### Analytics tools:

- Google Analytics for tracking website traffic from social media.
- Sprout Social or Hootsuite for detailed platform analytics.
- TikTok Analytics and Instagram Insights for specific post performance.

### Adapting to New Social Media Features

Social media platforms regularly roll out new features to keep users engaged. By adopting these features early, you can stay competitive and get a boost from algorithms that prioritize new tools.

### Example: Instagram Reels and TikTok Shorts

When Instagram introduced Reels and TikTok rolled out its Shorts feature, early adopters saw massive spikes in reach and engagement because the platforms were promoting these formats heavily. Today, short-form video is a dominant trend.

## What to do:

- Create content that fits new formats. For example, if Instagram releases a new feature (like Reels), make it part of your content plan.
- Experiment with these features in a way that aligns with your brand, whether it's showcasing behind-the-scenes moments, educational tips, or quick challenges.

## Example: Live Streaming

Platforms like Instagram, TikTok, and YouTube are pushing live streaming to drive real-time engagement. Early adopters have used this to build deeper connections with their audience and host events like product launches or Q&A sessions.

## Actionable steps:

- Schedule regular live sessions to interact with your audience.
- Test different formats like tutorials, AMAs (Ask Me Anything), or event recaps.
- Promote live streams in advance to ensure higher participation.

## Embracing the Future: AR, VR, and AI in Social Media

The future of social media is leaning heavily into new technologies like Augmented Reality (AR), Virtual Reality (VR), and Artificial Intelligence (AI). By understanding how these innovations are shaping the landscape, you can be ready to integrate them into your strategy.

## Augmented Reality (AR)

AR features are already transforming platforms like Snapchat and Instagram, with filters and interactive experiences that engage users in new ways. Brands that use AR effectively can create immersive experiences for their audience, making them more memorable.

### How to use AR:

- Create branded filters or AR effects that align with your messaging.
- Partner with creators who specialize in AR to develop engaging content.

## Virtual Reality (VR)

Though still in its early stages, VR is growing rapidly, particularly in spaces like gaming and immersive experiences. Facebook's parent company, Meta, is heavily investing in VR, signaling that it may become a central component of social media in the coming years.

### How to use VR:

- Consider how VR could enhance your storytelling or allow your audience to "experience" your brand.
- Explore platforms like Meta's Horizon Worlds to start experimenting with virtual spaces.

## Artificial Intelligence (AI)
AI-powered tools are becoming essential for content creation, from scheduling posts to analyzing trends. AI can help streamline your workflow and optimize your strategy for success.

## Examples of AI tools:
- ChatGPT or Jasper for content ideation and writing.
- Canva for AI-assisted design.
- Sprinklr for AI-powered social media analytics.

## Adapting to Algorithm Changes
Algorithm changes are inevitable, and they can either boost or damage your reach depending on how you adapt. Being reactive and adjusting your strategy when major changes happen is critical to maintaining engagement.

**Proactive Steps:**

**1. Diversify Your Content Types:** Instead of relying solely on one type of content (like photos or text posts), mix it up with videos, live streams, and interactive stories. This helps you stay visible even if the algorithm starts favoring a different format.

**2. Post Consistently:** Even when algorithms change, consistent posting signals to platforms that you're active and reliable. Create a consistent content schedule, so you're always in front of your audience.

**3. Engage Frequently:** Platforms reward engagement. Respond to comments, participate in conversations, and use features like polls or Q&A sessions to maintain an active presence.

**4. Stay Updated:** Follow blogs, newsletters, or join communities where algorithm changes are discussed. Being one of the first to adapt can give you a significant advantage.

## US-Based Example: How Netflix Uses Trend-Driven Content

Netflix is a great example of a brand that stays ahead of trends. By leveraging popular memes, creating timely social media campaigns, and responding in real time to conversations on Twitter, they consistently engage a global audience. They also use AI to recommend personalized content, showing how technology can help companies future-proof their marketing.

## Future-Proofing Your Social Media Strategy: Key Takeaways

- **Stay Curious:** Always be on the lookout for new tools, platforms, and content trends.
- **Adapt Quickly:** When you spot a trend or algorithm change, don't wait to incorporate it into your strategy.
- **Leverage New Technologies:** Whether it's AI tools, AR filters, or live streaming, using the latest technology can help you stand out.
- **Monitor Performance:** Use analytics to track how your strategy is performing and adjust where needed.
- **Engage Your Audience:** Building and maintaining engagement is the cornerstone of long-term social media success, no matter the platform.

The world of social media is always evolving, but with a proactive mindset and a flexible strategy, you'll be prepared to navigate whatever comes next. By staying up to date with trends, incorporating new technologies, and adapting quickly, you can ensure that your social media presence remains strong and relevant for years to come.

Your success lies in your ability to stay ahead, adapt, and consistently deliver content that resonates with your audience—no matter what the next big trend may be.

# Appendix A

# Social Media Platform Comparison for Creators and Entrepreneurs

When it comes to growing your personal brand or business, understanding the strengths and weaknesses of different social media platforms is crucial. Here's a breakdown of some of the most popular platforms, their core features, and how creators and entrepreneurs can best use them.

| Platform | Audience Demographics | Best for | Key Features | Monetization Opportunities |
|---|---|---|---|---|
| Instagram | 18-34 years, global research | Visual story telling, randing | Stories, Reels, IGTV, Shopping | Sponsored posts, affiliate links, product sales |
| TikTok | 16-24 years, fast-growing globally | Viral short-form video content | Challenges, trending audio, filters | Sponsored content, brand partnerships |
| Facebook | 25-45 years, wide demographic reach | Community building, ads | Groups, Marketplace, Facebook Ads | Facebook Ads, product sales, subscriptions |
| YouTube | All ages, video-focu | Long-form content, | Shorts, Live streaming, | Ad revenue, sponsored |

|  | sed | tutorials | memberships | videos, channel memberships |
|---|---|---|---|---|
| X (Twitter) | 18-49 years, real-time conversations | News, updates, engagement | Threads, trending topics, Spaces | Sponsored tweets, affiliate marketing |
| LinkedIn | 25-49 years, professionals | Networking, B2B marketing | Articles, job postings, LinkedIn Live | Sponsored content, product promotion, courses |

# Appendix B

# Content Calendar Template for Consistency

Creating a content calendar is one of the best ways to maintain a consistent posting schedule and ensure you're delivering valuable content to your audience regularly. Here's a simple template to help you plan and organize your content.

| Week | Platform | Content Type | Topic/Theme | Caption Ideas | Hashtags/Keywords | Date/Time of Post |
|---|---|---|---|---|---|---|
| 1 | Instagram | Image + Caption | Behind-the-scenes | "A peek behind the scenes..." | #BehindTheScenes #EntrepreneurLife | Monday, 9 AM |
| 1 | Tiktok | Short video | Product demo | "Check out our latest product!" | #Demo #NewProduct | Wednesday, 3 PM |
| 1 | Facebook | Long Post + Image | Industry insights | "Here's why this trend is changing the game..." | #BusinessTrends | Friday, 12 PM |

Use this template to plan for multiple weeks and across different platforms, making sure your content aligns with your goals and resonates with your audience.

# Appendix C

# Best Tools for Growing and Managing Your Social Media Pages

Managing multiple social media accounts and creating content can be overwhelming without the right tools. Here are some of the best tools that can help streamline your efforts and grow your social media presence:

| Tool | Purpose | Best For | Platform Support |
|------|---------|----------|------------------|
| Buffer | Scheduling posts across platforms | Consistent posting, content calendar | Instagram, Facebook, Twitter, LinkedIn |
| Canva | Creating stunning visuals | Designing social media graphics | All major platforms |
| Later | Instagram and TikTok scheduling, analytics | Instagram growth, hashtag suggestions | Instagram, TikTok |
| Hootsuite | Social media management | Managing multiple accounts, analytics | All major platforms |

| | | | |
|---|---|---|---|
| Sprout Social | Analytics and reporting | Tracking engagement, ROI | Instagram, Facebook, Twitter, LinkedIn |
| TubeBuddy | YouTube optimization | Improving SEO, tracking channel growth | YouTube |

These tools help with everything from content creation to analytics, making it easier to grow and manage your social media pages.

# Appendix D

## Inspiring Stories from Creators Who Monetized Their Social Media Fame

Many creators have turned their passion for social media into a full-time income, often using innovative strategies to monetize their influence. Here are a few stories to inspire you:

### 1. Zach King (Instagram/ TikTok/ YouTube)

Known for his viral "magic" videos, Zach King started as a YouTuber and quickly grew on other platforms. Today, he collaborates with brands for sponsored content, and his videos regularly attract millions of views. He leveraged his storytelling skills to make content that resonates with a global audience.

### 2. Patricia Bright (YouTube/Instagram)

Patricia Bright began as a beauty and lifestyle YouTuber and has since grown her personal brand to include partnerships with major brands like MAC Cosmetics and L'Oréal. She also created her own courses to teach others how to grow their influence online, diversifying her revenue streams.

### 3. Charli D'Amelio (TikTok/Instagram)

Charli D'Amelio skyrocketed to fame through TikTok's viral dance challenges, amassing millions of followers. She's since built a brand around her personality, securing major endorsement deals, launching her own merchandise line, and even starring in family reality TV.

These stories show the power of building a community and leveraging your personal brand to unlock monetization opportunities, from brand deals to launching your own products.